Contents

1. Why Prayer Is Important to God 7

2. Putting God to Work 21

3. The Necessity for Praying People 41

4. God's Need for People Who Pray 53

5. Prayerless Christians 63

6. Praying for Others 75

7. Preachers and Prayer 85

8. Prayerlessness in the Pulpit 105

9. Equipped by Prayer 121

10. The Preacher's Cry: "Pray for Us!" 139

11. Modern Examples of Prayer 153

12. More Modern Examples of Prayer 175

THE
WEAPON
OF
PRAYER

Life of power
is two to through
prayer and fasting
and God's word

E.M. BOUNDS

🔲 *Whitaker House*

Unless otherwise indicated, all Scripture quotations are from the *King James Version* (KJV) of the Bible.

Scripture quotations marked (RV) are taken from the *Revised Version* of the Holy Bible.

Scripture quotations marked (RSV) are from the *Revised Standard Version Common Bible* © 1973, by the Division of Christian Education of the National Council of Churches of Christ in the U.S.A. Used by permission.

THE WEAPON OF PRAYER

ISBN: 0-88368-457-8
Printed in the United States of America
Copyright © 1996 by Whitaker House

Whitaker House
30 Hunt Valley Circle
New Kensington, PA 15068

4 5 6 7 8 9 10 11 / 06 05 04 03 02 01 00 99 98

Chapter One

Why Prayer Is Important to God

Then shalt thou call, and the LORD shall answer; thou shalt cry, and he shall say, Here I am. Then shalt thou delight thyself in the LORD; and I will cause thee to ride upon the high places of the earth, and feed thee with the heritage of Jacob thy father: for the mouth of the LORD hath spoken it. —Isaiah 58:9, 14

It must never be forgotten that almighty God rules this world. He is not an absentee God. His hand is always on the controls of human affairs. He is present everywhere in the concerns of time. "His eyes behold, his eyelids try, the children of men" (Ps. 11:4). He rules the world just as He rules the church— through prayer. This lesson needs to be taught and taught again to men and women. Then this lesson will affect the consciences of those whose eyes have no vision for eternal things, whose ears are deaf toward God.

LK 18:1   In dealing with mankind, nothing is more important to God than prayer. Prayer is likewise of great importance to people. Failure to pray is failure in all of life. It is failure of duty, service, and spiritual progress. It is only by prayer that God can help people. He who does not pray, therefore, robs himself of God's help and places God where He cannot help people.

We must pray to God if love for God is to exist. Faith and hope and patience and all the strong, beautiful, vital forces of piety are withered and dead in a prayerless life. An individual believer's life, his personal salvation, and his personal Christian graces have their being, bloom, and fruit in prayer.

All this and much more can be said about how prayer is necessary to the life and piety of the individual. But prayer has a larger sphere, a loftier inspiration, a higher duty. Prayer concerns God, whose purposes and plans are conditioned on prayer. His will and His glory are bound up in praying. The days of God's splendor and renown have always been the great days of prayer. God's great movements in this world have been conditioned on, continued by, and fashioned by prayer. God has put Himself in these great movements just as men and women have prayed. Present, prevailing, conspicuous, and overcoming prayer has always brought God's presence. The real and obvious test of a genuine work of God is the prevalence of the spirit of prayer. God's mightiest forces fill and permeate a movement when prayer's mightiest forces are there.

God's movement to bring Israel from Egyptian bondage had its inception in prayer. (See Exodus 2:23–25; 3:9.) Thus, it was early in history when God made prayer one of the granite forces upon which His world movements would be based.

Hannah's petition for a son (1 Sam. 1:11) began a great prayer movement for God in Israel. Praying women, like Hannah, whose prayers can give men like Samuel to the cause of God, do more for the church and the world than all the politicians on earth. People born of prayer are the saviors of the state, and people saturated with prayer give life and impetus to the church. Under God they are saviors and helpers of both church and state.

We must believe that the divine record about prayer and God is given in order that we might be constantly reminded of Him. And we are ever refreshed by the knowledge that God holds His church and that God's purpose will be fulfilled. His plans concerning the church will most assuredly and inevitably be carried out. That record of God has been given without doubt; therefore, we may be deeply impressed that the prayers of God's saints are a great factor, a supreme factor, in carrying forward God's work with ease and in time. When the church is in the condition of prayer, God's cause always flourishes, and His kingdom on earth always triumphs. When the church fails to pray, God's cause decays, and evil of every kind prevails.

In other words, God works through the prayers of His people, and when they fail Him at this point, decline and deadness follow. It is according to the divine plan that spiritual prosperity comes through the prayer channel. Praying saints are God's agents for carrying on His saving and providential work on earth. If His agents fail Him, neglecting to pray, then His work fails. Praying agents of the Most High are always forerunners of spiritual prosperity.

In all ages, those who have led the church of God have had a full and rich ministry of prayer. In the Bible, the rulers of the church had preeminence in prayer. They may have been eminent in culture, intellect, and all human abilities, or they may have been lowly in physical attainments and natural gifts. Yet, in each case prayer was the all-powerful force in the leadership of the church. This was so because God was with them in what they did, for prayer always carries us back to God. It recognizes God and brings God into the world to work and to save and to bless. The most effective agents in spreading the knowledge of God, in performing His work on the earth, and in standing as a barrier against the billows of evil, have been praying church leaders. God depends on them, employs them, and blesses them.

Prayer cannot be retired as a secondary force in this world. To do so is to retire God from moving in our lives. It is to make God secondary. The prayer ministry is an all-engaging force; it must be all-engaging to be a force at all. Prayer is the sense of a need for God and the call for God's help to supply that need. How we estimate and place prayer is how we estimate and place God. To give prayer a secondary place is to make God secondary in life's affairs. To substitute other forces for prayer excludes God and materializes the whole movement.

Prayer is absolutely necessary if we want to carry on God's work properly. God has intended it to be so. The Twelve in the early church knew the importance of prayer. In fact, when they heard the complaint that certain widows had been neglected in the daily distribution, they did not handle it all by themselves. (See Acts 6:1–2.) The Twelve called all the disciples together and told them to select seven men, "full of the Holy Ghost and wisdom" (Acts 6:3), whom they would appoint over that benevolent work. They added this important statement: "But we will give ourselves continually to prayer, and to the ministry of the word" (Acts 6:4). They surely realized that the success of the Word and the progress of the church were dependent in a preeminent sense on their giving themselves to prayer. God could effectively work through them in proportion to how much they gave themselves to prayer.

The apostles were as dependent on prayer as everyone else. Sacred work, or church activities, may make us so busy that they hinder praying; and when this is the case, evil always results. It is better to let the work go by default than to let the praying go by neglect. Whatever affects the intensity of our praying affects the value of our work. "Too busy to pray" is not only the keynote to backsliding, but it mars even the work that is done.

Nothing is done well without prayer for the simple reason that it leaves God out of the work. It is so easy to be seduced by the good to the neglect of the best, until both the good and the best perish. How easily believers, even leaders of the church, are led by the deceptive wiles of Satan to cut short their praying in the interests of the work! How easy it is to neglect prayer or abbreviate our praying simply by the excuse that we have church work on our hands. When he can keep us too busy to stop and pray, Satan has effectively disarmed us.

"We will give ourselves continually to prayer, and to the ministry of the word" (Acts 6:4). The Revised Version states, "We will continue stedfastly in prayer." The implication of the word "continue" is to be strong, steadfast, to be devoted to, to keep at it with constant care, to make a business out of it. We find the same word in Colossians 4:2, which reads, "Continue in prayer, and watch in the same with thanksgiving." We also find it in Romans 12:12, which is translated, "Continuing instant in prayer."

The apostles were under the law of prayer. This law recognizes God as God and depends on Him to do what He would not do without prayer. They were under the necessity of prayer, just as all believers are, in every age and in every place. They had to be devoted to prayer in order to make their ministry of the Word effective. The business of preaching is worth very little unless it is in direct partnership with the business of praying. Apostolic preaching cannot be carried on unless there is apostolic praying.

Alas, this plain truth has been easily forgotten by those who minister in holy things! Without in any way passing a criticism on the ministry, I feel it is high time that somebody declared to ministers that effective preaching cannot take place without effective praying. The preaching that is most successful comes from a ministry that prays much. Perhaps one might go so far as to say that such a ministry is the only kind that is successful. God can mightily use the preacher who prays. He is God's chosen messenger for good, and the Holy Spirit delights to honor him. A praying preacher is God's effective agent in saving sinners and in edifying saints.

In Acts 6:1–8 we have the record of how, long ago, the apostles felt that they were losing—indeed, had lost—apostolic power because they were involved in certain duties that prevented them from praying more. So they called everything to a halt. They had discovered, to their regret, that they were too deficient in praying. Doubtless, they had kept up the form of praying, but it was seriously lacking in intensity and in the amount of time given to it. Their minds were too preoccupied with the finances of the church.

Likewise, even in the church today, we find both laymen and ministers so busily engaged in "serving" that they are glaringly

14

deficient in praying. In fact, in present-day church affairs, people are considered religious if they give largely of their money to the church; and people are chosen for official positions, not because they are people of prayer, but because they have the ability to run church finances and to get money for the church.

Now, when these apostles looked into this matter, they determined to put aside these hindrances resulting from church finances, and they resolved to give themselves to prayer. Not that these finances were to be ignored or set aside, but ordinary laymen, "full of faith and of the Holy Ghost" (Acts 6:5), could work with the finances. These men were to be truly religious men who could easily attend to these financial matters without it affecting their piety or their praying in the least. They would thus have something to do in the church, and at the same time they could take the burden off of the apostles. In turn, the apostles would be able to pray more. Praying more, they themselves would be blessed in soul, and they would be more effective in the work to which they had been called.

The apostles realized, too, as they had not realized before, that they were being so pressured by attention to material things, things right in themselves, that they could not pray fully. They could not give to prayer that strength, zeal, and time that its nature and importance demand.

Likewise, we will discover, under close scrutiny of ourselves sometimes, that legitimate and commendable things may so engross our attention that prayer is omitted, or at least very little time is given to it.

How easy to slip away from the prayer closet! Even the apostles had to guard themselves at that point. How closely we need to watch ourselves at the same place! Things legitimate and right may become wrong when they take the place of prayer. Things right in themselves may become wrong things when they are allowed to fasten themselves excessively upon our hearts. It is not only the sinful things that hurt prayer. It is not only questionable things that are to be guarded against, but it is also things which are right in their places but which are allowed to sidetrack prayer and shut the door of the prayer closet, often with the self-comforting plea that "we are too busy to pray."

Possibly, busyness has had as much to do with the breaking down of family prayer in this age as any other cause. Busyness has caused family religion to decay, and busyness is one cause of the decline of the prayer meeting. Men and women are too busy with legitimate things to give themselves to prayer. Other things are given the right-of-way. Prayer is set aside. Business comes first. And this does not always mean that prayer is second, but oftentimes prayer is left out entirely.

The apostles tackled this problem, and they determined that not even church business would affect their praying habits. Prayer had to come first; then they would be God's real agents in His world, in deed and truth. God could work effectively through them because they prayed and thereby put themselves directly in line with His plans and purposes. And His plan and purpose is to work through people who pray.

When the complaint about the daily distribution came to the apostles' ears, they discovered that their work had not been accomplishing fully the divine ends of peace, gratitude, and unity. On the contrary, discontent, complaining, and division were the result of their work, which had far too little prayer in it. So, they promptly restored prayer to its rightful prominence.

Praying men and women are a necessity in carrying out God's plan for saving sinners. God has made it so. God established prayer as a divine ordinance, and therefore we are to pray. The fact that God has so often employed men and women of prayer to accomplish His plans clearly proves we are to pray. It is unnecessary to name all the instances in which God used the prayers of righteous men and women to carry out His gracious designs. Time and space are too limited for the list. However, I will name one or two cases.

In the case of the golden calf, God purposed to destroy the Israelites because of their great sin of idolatry. (See Deuteronomy 9:12–21.) While Moses was receiving the law at God's hands, Aaron was swept away by the strong, popular tide of unbelief and sin. The very being of Israel was imperiled. All seemed lost except Moses and prayer, and prayer became more effective and wonder-working on behalf of Israel than Aaron's magic rod. God determined to destroy Israel and Aaron, for His anger grew hot. It was a fearful and critical hour. But prayer was the levee that held back heaven's desolating fury. God's hand was held fast by the prayers of Moses, the mighty intercessor.

Moses was set on delivering Israel. He prayed for forty days and forty nights; it was a long and exhaustive struggle. Not for one moment did he relax his hold on God. Not for one moment did he leave his place at the feet of God, even for food. Not for one moment did he moderate his demand or ease his cry. Israel's existence was in the balance. The wrath of almighty God had to be stayed. Israel had to be saved at all cost. And Israel *was* saved. Moses would not let God alone. And so, today, we can look back and give the credit for the present race of the Jews to the praying of Moses centuries ago.

Persevering prayer always wins; God yields to persistence and fidelity. He has no heart to say no to praying such as Moses did. God's purpose to destroy Israel was actually changed by the praying of this man of God. This illustrates how much just one praying person is worth in this world, and how much depends on him.

Daniel, in Babylon, refused to obey the decree of the king. (See Daniel 6:1–23.) The king had decreed that no one could ask any petition of any god or man for thirty days. But Daniel shut his eyes to the decree that would shut him off from his prayer room; he refused to allow fear of consequences to deter him from calling on God. So, he "kneeled upon his knees three times a day" (Dan. 6:10) and prayed as he had done before, putting in God's hands all the consequences of disobeying the king.

There was nothing impersonal about Daniel's praying. It always had an objective, and it was an appeal to a great God who could do all things. Daniel did not pamper himself or look for a feeling to urge him to pray. In the face of the dreadful decree that could hurl him from his high position into the lion's den, "he kneeled upon his knees three times a day... and gave thanks before his God, as he did aforetime" (Dan. 6:10). The gracious result was that prayer laid its hands upon an almighty arm, which intervened in that den of vicious lions. God closed their mouths and preserved His servant Daniel, who had been true to Him and who had called on Him for protection.

Daniel's praying was an essential factor in defeating the king's decree and in defeating the wicked, envious rulers who had tried to trap him. They wanted to destroy him and remove him from his powerful position in the kingdom, but Daniel's prayers prevailed!

Chapter Two

Putting God to Work

From of old no one has heard or perceived by the ear, no eye has seen a God besides thee, who works for those who wait for him.

—Isaiah 64:4 (RSV)

When I use the expression, "putting God to work," I mean that God has placed Himself under the law of prayer and has obligated Himself to answer prayer. God has ordained prayer, and He will do things through people as they pray that He would not do otherwise. Prayer is a specific, divine appointment, an ordinance of heaven. By prayer, God purposes to carry out His gracious designs on earth and to execute and make effective the plan of salvation.

When I say that prayer puts God to work, I am simply saying that we have it in our power to move God to work by prayer. Prayer moves God to do works among people—in His own way, of course—that He would not do if the prayers were not made. Thus, while prayer moves God to work, at the same time God puts prayer to work. Since God has ordained prayer, and since prayer involves people and has no existence apart from people, then logically people's prayers are the one force that puts God to work in human affairs.

As we allude to prayer and read about prayer in the Scriptures, let us keep in mind these fundamental truths.

If prayer puts God to work on earth, then, by the same token, prayerlessness excludes God from the world's affairs and prevents Him from working. If prayer moves God to work in this world's affairs, then prayerlessness excludes God from everything concerning people. Prayerlessness leaves man as the mere creature of circumstances, at the mercy of blind fate, and without help of any kind from God. It leaves man with the tremendous responsibilities and difficult problems of the world, with all of its sorrows and burdens and afflictions, without any God at all. In reality, the denial of prayer is the denial of God Himself, for God and prayer are so inseparable that they can never be divorced.

Prayer affects three different spheres of existence: the divine, the angelic, and the human. It puts God to work, it puts angels to work, and it puts people to work. It lays its hands upon God, angels, and people. What a wonderful reach there is in prayer! It brings into play the forces of heaven and earth. God, angels, and people are subjects of this wonderful law of prayer, and all three deal with the possibilities and the results of prayer.

God has placed Himself under the law of prayer to such an extent that He is induced to work among people in a way in which He does not work if they do not pray. Prayer takes hold of God and influences Him to work. This is the meaning of prayer as it concerns God. This is the doctrine of prayer, or else there is no value whatsoever in prayer.

Prayer puts God to work in all things prayed for. While man in his weakness and poverty waits, trusts, and prays, God undertakes the work. "From of old no one has heard or perceived by the ear, no eye has seen a God besides thee, who works for those who wait for him" (Isa. 64:4 RSV).

Jesus Christ commits Himself to the force of prayer. "Whatsoever ye shall ask in my name," He says, "that will I do, that the Father may be glorified in the Son. If ye shall ask any thing in my name, I will do it" (John 14:13–14). And, again, "If ye abide in me, and my words abide in you, ye shall ask what ye will, and it shall be done unto you" (John 15:7).

The promise of God is committed to nothing as strongly as it is to prayer. The purposes of God are not dependent on any other force as much as this force of prayer. The Word of God expounds on the necessity and results of prayer. The work of God halts or advances according to the strength of prayer. Prophets and apostles have urged the utility, force, and necessity of prayer. For example, Isaiah 62:6–7 says,

> *I have set watchmen upon thy walls, O Jerusalem, which shall never hold their peace day nor night: ye that make mention of the LORD, keep not silence. And give him no rest, till he establish, and till he make Jerusalem a praise in the earth.*

(an tī sēd'nt)

Prayer, with its antecedents and attendants, is the one and only condition of the final triumph of the Gospel. The fact that it is the one and only condition honors the Father and glorifies the Son. Little praying and poor praying have weakened Christ's power on earth, postponed the glorious results of His reign, and retired God from His sovereignty.

Prayer puts God's work in His hands and keeps it there. It looks to Him constantly and depends on Him implicitly to further His own

antecedent- Going before, preceding one that precedes

cause. Prayer is simply faith resting in, acting with, leaning on, and obeying God. This is why God loves it so well, why He puts all power into its hands, and why He so highly esteems people of prayer.

Every movement for the advancement of the Gospel must be created by and inspired by prayer. Prayer precedes and accompanies all the movements of God as an invariable and necessary condition.

In this sense, God makes prayer identical in force and power with Himself, and He says to those on earth who pray, "You are on the earth to carry on My cause. I am in heaven, the Lord of all, the Maker of all, the Holy One of all. Now whatever you need for My cause, ask Me, and I will do it. Shape the future by your prayers, and concerning all that you need for present supplies, command Me (Isa. 45:11). I made heaven and earth and all things in them (Acts 14:15). Ask for great things. 'Open thy mouth wide, and I will fill it' (Ps. 81:10). It is My work that you are doing. It concerns My cause. Be prompt and full in praying. Do not abate your asking, and I will not wince or abate My giving."

Everywhere in His Word, God bases His actions on prayer. Everywhere in His Word, His actions and attitude are shaped by prayer. To quote all the scriptural passages that prove the direct relationship of prayer to God, would be to transfer whole pages of the Bible to this study. Man has personal relations with God, and prayer is the divinely appointed means by which man comes into direct connection with God. By His own ordinance, God binds Himself to hear our prayers. God bestows His great blessings on His children when they seek them along the avenue of prayer.

When Solomon closed his great prayer that he offered at the dedication of the temple, God appeared to him, approved him, and laid down the universal principles of His actions. In 2 Chronicles 7:12-15 we read as follows:

> And the LORD appeared to Solomon by night, and said unto him, I have heard thy prayer, and have chosen this place to myself for an house of sacrifice. If I shut up heaven that there be no rain, or if I command the locusts to devour the land, or if I send pestilence among my people; If my people, which are called by my name, shall humble themselves, and pray, and seek my face, and turn from their wicked ways; then will I hear from heaven, and will forgive their sin, and will heal their land. Now mine eyes shall be open, and mine ears attent unto the prayer that is made in this place.

In His purposes concerning the Jews in the Babylonian captivity, God asserts His unfailing principles:

> *For thus saith the LORD, That after seventy years be accomplished at Babylon I will visit you, and perform my good word toward you, in causing you to return to this place. For I know the thoughts that I think toward you, saith the LORD, thoughts of peace, and not of evil, to give you an expected end. Then shall ye call upon me, and ye shall go and pray unto me, and I will hearken unto you. And ye shall seek me, and find me, when ye shall search for me with all your heart.* (Jer. 29:10–13)

In Bible terminology, prayer means calling on God for things we desire, asking God for things. Thus, we read, "Call unto me, and I will answer thee, and show thee great and mighty things, which thou knowest not" (Jer. 33:3). "Call upon me in the day of trouble: I will deliver thee" (Ps. 50:15). "Then shalt thou call, and the LORD shall answer; thou shalt cry, and he shall say, Here I am" (Isa. 58:9).

Prayer is revealed as a direct application to God for some temporal or spiritual good. It is an appeal to God to intervene in life's affairs

27

for the good of those for whom we pray. God is recognized as the source and fountain of all good, and prayer implies that all His good is held in His keeping for those who call on Him in truth.

The fact that prayer is an appeal to God, communication with God, and communion with God, comes out strongly and simply in the praying of Old Testament saints. Abraham's intercession for Sodom is a striking illustration of the nature of prayer. (See Genesis 18:20–33; 19:24–25.) It is an example of communication with God and intercession for man. Abraham encountered God's plan to destroy Sodom, and his soul within him was greatly moved because of his great interest in that fated city. His nephew and family resided there. God's purpose to destroy the city had to be changed; God's decree to destroy its evil inhabitants had to be revoked.

It was no small undertaking that faced Abraham when he decided to beseech God to spare Sodom. Abraham set about to change God's purpose and to save Sodom along with the other cities of the plain. It was certainly a most difficult and delicate work for him—to undertake using his influence with God to save those doomed cities.

He used the plea that there may be righteous people in Sodom, and he appealed to the infinite uprightness of God not to destroy the righteous with the wicked: "That be far from thee to do after this manner, to slay the righteous with the wicked...Shall not the Judge of all the earth do right?" (Gen. 18:25). With what deep self-abasement and reverence did Abraham begin his high and divine work! He stood before God in solemn awe and meditation, and then he drew near to God and spoke. He asked God to spare Sodom if there were fifty righteous people in the city, and he kept reducing the number until it was down to ten. He advanced step by step in faith, in demand, and in urgency, and God granted every request that he made.

It has been well said that Abraham stopped asking before God stopped granting. It seems that Abraham had a kind of optimistic view of the piety of Sodom. He scarcely expected when he undertook this matter to have it end in failure. He was very much in earnest, and he had every encouragement to press his case. When he made his final request, he thought that surely with Lot, his wife, his daughters, his sons, and his sons-in-law, he had his ten righteous people for whose sake God would spare the city. But, alas! The count failed when the final test came. There were not ten righteous people in that large population.

In his goodness of heart, Abraham overestimated the number of pious people in that city. Otherwise, God might possibly have saved it if he had reduced his figures still further. But this much is true: even if he did not save Sodom by his persistent praying, the purposes of God were postponed for a season.

This is a representative case of Old Testament praying, and it discloses God's mode of working through prayer. It further shows how God is moved to work in this world in answer to prayer, even when it comes to changing His purposes concerning a sinful community. This praying of Abraham was no mere performance—no dull, lifeless ceremony—but an earnest plea, a strong entreaty, one person with another Person. Its purpose was to have an influence, to secure a desired end.

How full of meaning is this remarkable series of intercessions made by Abraham! Here we have arguments designed to convince God; here we have pleas to persuade God to change His purpose. We see deep humility, but we see holy boldness and perseverance as well. We see how Abraham kept advancing in his requests because God kept granting each petition. Here we have large requests encouraged by large answers. God stays and answers as long as Abraham stays and asks. To Abraham, God is existent, approachable, and all-powerful; furthermore, He defers to people, acts favorably on their desires, and grants them favors asked for. Not to pray is to deny God—to deny His existence, His nature, and His purposes toward mankind.

God has given us specific prayer promises and has outlined their breadth, certainty, and limitations. Jesus Christ urges us into the presence of God with these prayer promises by the assurance not only that God will answer, but that no other being but God can answer. He urges us toward God because only by prayer can we move God to take a hand in earth's affairs and induce Him to intervene on our behalf.

Jesus said, "All things, whatsoever ye shall ask in prayer, believing, ye shall receive" (Matt. 21:22). This all-inclusive condition not only urges us to pray for all things, everything great and small, but it points us to and limits us to God. Who but God can cover the whole range of universal things? Who but God gives us the whole thesaurus of earthly and heavenly good from which to ask? Who but God can assure us with certainty that we will receive the very thing for which we ask?

It is Jesus Christ, the Son of God, who commands us to pray, and it is He who puts Himself and all He has so fully in the answer. It is He who puts Himself at our service and answers our demands when we pray. Jesus puts Himself and the Father at our command in prayer; He promises to come directly into our lives and to work for our good. Also, He promises to answer the demands of two or more believers who agree in prayer about any one thing.

> *If two of you shall agree on earth as touching any thing that they shall ask, it shall be done for them of my Father which is in heaven.*   *(Matt. 18:19)*

None but God could put Himself in a covenant so binding as that, for only God could fulfill such a promise and reach to its exacting and all-controlling demands. Only God can keep these promises.

God needs prayer, and people need prayer, too. It is indispensable to God's work in this world, and it is essential to getting God to work in earth's affairs. So, God binds people to pray by the most solemn obligations. God commands people to pray; therefore, not to pray is plain disobedience to an imperative command of almighty God. Prayer is such a prerequisite that the graces, the salvation, and the good of God are not bestowed on us unless we pray. Prayer is a high privilege, a royal prerogative. Manifold and eternal are the losses if we fail to exercise it. Prayer is the great, universal force that advances God's cause, the reverence that hallows God's name, and the establishment of God's kingdom in human hearts. These are created and affected by prayer.

One of the essential fortifiers of the Gospel is prayer. Without prayer, the Gospel can neither be preached effectively, proclaimed faithfully, experienced in the heart, nor practiced in the life. The reason is very simple: by leaving prayer out of the catalog of religious duties, we leave God out, too, and His work cannot progress without Him.

The things God purposed to do under King Cyrus of Persia, prophesied by Isaiah many years before Cyrus was born, were conditioned on prayer. God declares His purpose, power, independence, and defiance of obstacles, but His people still must pray. His omnipotent and absolutely infinite power encourages prayer. He has been ordering all events, directing all conditions, and creating all things so that He might answer prayer, and then He turns Himself over to His praying ones to be commanded. Then all the results and power He holds in His hands will be bestowed in lavish and unmeasured generosity to answer prayers and to make prayer the mightiest energy in the world.

The passage concerning Cyrus in Isaiah 45 is too lengthy to be quoted in its entirety, but it is well worth reading. It closes with strong words about prayer, words that are the climax of all that God says concerning His purposes in connection with Cyrus:

> *Thus saith the LORD, the Holy One of Israel, and his Maker, Ask me of things to come concerning my sons, and concerning the work of my hands command ye me. I have made the earth, and created man upon it: I, even my hands, have stretched out the heavens, and all their host have I commanded. (Isa. 45:11–12)*

The book of Job also tells of the importance of prayer. In the conclusion of the story of Job, we see how God intervenes on behalf of Job and tells his friends to present themselves before Job so that he may pray for them. "My wrath is kindled against thee [Eliphaz], and against thy two friends" (Job 42:7) is God's statement, with the further words added, "My servant Job shall pray for you: for him will I accept" (Job 42:8). It is a striking illustration of God intervening to deliver Job's friends in answer to Job's prayer.

I have heretofore spoken of prayer affecting God, angels, and people. Christ wrote no books while living. Memoranda, notes, sermon-writing, and sermon-making were alien to Him. Autobiography was not to His taste. The revelation to John was His last utterance. In the book of Revelation, we have a depiction of the great importance, the priceless value, and the high position that prayer has in the progress of God's church in the world. This depiction reveals the angels' interest in the prayers of the saints and in accomplishing the answers to those prayers:

> *And another angel came and stood at the altar, having a golden censer; and there was given unto him much incense, that he should offer it with the prayers of all saints upon the golden altar which was before the throne. And the smoke of the incense, which came with the prayers of the saints, ascended up before God out of the angel's hand. And the angel took the censer, and filled it with fire of the altar, and cast it into the earth: and there were voices, and thunderings, and lightnings, and an earthquake.*
>
> *(Rev 8:3–5)*

Translated into the prose of everyday life, these words show how the business of salvation is carried on by and made up of the prayers of God's saints on earth. The passage discloses how these prayers come back to earth in flaming power and produce mighty commotions, influences, and revolutions.

Praying men and women are essential to almighty God in all His plans and purposes. God's plans, secrets, and cause have never been committed to prayerless people. Neglect of prayer has always brought loss of faith and loss of love. Failure to pray has been the destructive, inevitable cause of backsliding and estrangement from God. Prayerless people have stood in the way of God fulfilling His Word and doing His will on earth. They tie the divine hands and interfere with God in His gracious designs. As praying people are a help to God, so prayerless people are a hindrance to Him.

I stress the scriptural view of the necessity of prayer even at the cost of repeating myself. The subject is too important for repetition to weaken or tire, too vital to be trite or tame. We must feel it anew. The fires of prayer have burned low. Ashes, not flames, are on its altars.

No insistence in the Scriptures is more pressing than that we must pray. No exhortation is more often reiterated, none is more hearty, none is more solemn and stirring, than to pray. No principle is more strongly and broadly declared than that which urges us to pray. There is no duty to which we are more strongly obliged than that of praying. There is no command more imperative and insistent than that of praying. Are you praying in everything without ceasing (1 Thess. 5:17)? Are you praying in your prayer closet, hidden from the eyes of others? Are you praying always and everywhere? These are personal, pertinent, and all-important questions for every soul.

God's Word shows us, through many examples, that God intervenes in this world in answer to prayer. How clear it is, when the Bible is consulted, that the almighty God is brought directly into the things of this world by the prayers of His people. Jonah fled from duty and took ship for a distant port, but God followed him. By a strange providence this disobedient prophet was cast out of the ship, and the God who sent him to Nineveh prepared a fish to swallow him. In the fish's belly he cried out to the God against whom he had sinned, and God intervened and caused the fish to vomit Jonah out onto dry land. Even the fishes of the great deep are subject to the law of prayer.

Likewise, the birds of the air are subject to this same law. Elijah had foretold to Ahab the coming of a prolonged drought, and food and water became scarce. God sent him to the brook Cherith and said to him,

It shall be, that thou shalt drink of the brook; and I have commanded the ravens

> *to feed thee there. And the ravens*
> *brought him bread and flesh in the*
> *morning, and bread and flesh in the*
> *evening; and he drank of the brook.*
>
> > *(1 Kings 17:4, 6)*

This is a man who later shut and opened the rain clouds by prayer. Can anyone doubt that this man of God was praying at this time, when so much was at stake? God intervened through the birds of the air this time, and He strangely moved them to take care of His servant so that he would not lack food and water.

David, in an evil hour, instead of listening to the advice of Joab, his prime minister, yielded to the suggestion of Satan. (See 1 Chronicles 21:1–14.) He took a census, thus displeasing God. So, God told him to choose one of three evils as a retribution for his folly and sin. He chose pestilence. Pestilence came among the people in violent form, and David went to prayer.

> *And David said unto God, Is it not I that*
> *commanded the people to be numbered?*
> *even I it is that have sinned and done evil*
> *indeed; but as for these sheep, what have*
> *they done? let thine hand, I pray thee, O*
> *LORD my God, be on me, and on my fa-*
> *ther's house; but not on thy people, that*
> *they should be plagued. (1 Chron. 21:17)*

Although God had been greatly grieved by David's sin, He could not resist this appeal from a penitent and prayerful spirit. God was moved by prayer to put His hand on the springs of disease and stop the fearful plague. God was put to work by David's prayer.

Numbers of other cases could be named, but these are sufficient. God seems to have taken great pains in His Word to show how He interferes in human affairs in answer to the prayers of His saints.

At this point a question might arise in some overcritical minds about the so-called "laws of nature." Those who raise this question are not strong believers in prayer; they think there is a conflict between what they call the laws of nature and the law of prayer. These people make nature a sort of imaginary god entirely separate from the almighty God. What is nature anyway? It is but the creation of God, the Maker of all things. And what are the laws of nature but the laws of God, through which He governs the material world? Since the law of prayer is also the law of God, there cannot possibly be any conflict between the two sets of laws, but prayer and nature must work in perfect harmony.

Prayer does not violate any natural law. God may set aside one law for the higher working of another law, and this He may do when He answers prayer. Or, God may answer prayer by working through the course of natural law. But, whether we understand it or not, God is over and above all nature. He can and will answer prayer in a wise, intelligent, and just manner, even though man may not comprehend it. So, in no sense is there any conflict between God's different laws when God intervenes in human affairs in answer to prayer.

Along this line of thought, another word might be said. I wrote something to which there can be no objection: prayer accomplishes things. However, it is not prayer itself that accomplishes things, but it is God working through it. Prayer is the instrument; God is the active agent. Prayer itself does not interfere in earth's affairs, but prayer moves God to intervene and do things. Prayer moves God to do things that He would not otherwise do.

It is like saying, "faith hath saved thee" (Luke 7:50). This simply means that God, through the faith of the sinner, saves him, faith being only the instrument that brings salvation to him.

Chapter Three

The Necessity for Praying People

Praying always with all prayer and supplication in the Spirit, and watching thereunto with all perseverance and supplication for all saints.
—*Ephesians 6:18*

Withal praying also for us, that God would open unto us a door of utterance, to speak the mystery of Christ, for which I am also in bonds: That I may make it manifest, as I ought to speak.
—*Colossians 4:3–4*

One of the most pressing needs in our day is for people whose faith, prayers, and study of the Word of God have been vitalized. We need people whose hearts have written on them a transcript of the Word. We need people who will give forth the Word as the incorruptible seed that lives and abides forever (1 Pet. 1:23).

A critical unbelief has eclipsed the Word of God. Nothing more is needed to clear up this haze than for the pulpit to pledge unwavering allegiance to the Bible and to fearlessly proclaim its truth. Without this the preacher fails, and his congregation becomes confused and unstable. The pulpit has done its mightiest work in the days of its unswerving loyalty to the Word of God.

In close connection with this, we must have preachers of prayer, preachers in high and low places who hold to and practice scriptural praying. While the pulpit must hold to its unswerving loyalty to the Word of God, it must, at the same time, be loyal to the doctrine of prayer, which that same Word illustrates and enforces upon mankind.

Christian schools, colleges, and education, considered simply as such, cannot be regarded as leaders in carrying forward the work of God's kingdom in the world. They have neither the right, the will, nor the power to do the work. This is to be accomplished by the preached Word, delivered in the power of the Holy Spirit sent down from heaven, sown with prayerful hands, and watered with the tears of praying hearts. This is the divine law, and we must follow it. We will follow the Lord.

~ Men and women are needed for the great work of soul-saving, and they are commanded to go (Mark 16:15). It is no angelic or impersonal force that is needed. Human hearts baptized with the spirit of prayer must bear the burden of this message. Human tongues on fire as the result of earnest, persistent prayer must declare the Word of God to dying people.

The church today needs praying people to meet the fearful crisis that is facing her. The crying need of the times is for people in increased numbers—God-fearing people, praying people, Holy Spirit people, people who can endure hardship. We need people who will not count their lives dear unto themselves (Acts 20:24) but count all things as loss for the excellency of the knowledge of Jesus Christ, the Savior (Phil. 3:8). The people who are so greatly needed in this age of the church are those who have learned the business of praying—learned it on their knees, learned it in the need and agony of their own hearts.

Praying people are the one commanding need of this day, as of all other days, if God is to intervene in the world. People who pray are, in reality, the only religious people. People of prayer are the only people who can, and do, represent God in this world. No cold, irreligious, prayerless person can claim the right.

He misrepresents God in all His work and all His plans.

Praying people are the only people who have influence with God, the only people to whom God commits Himself and His Gospel. Praying people are the only people in whom the Holy Spirit dwells, for the Holy Spirit and prayer go hand in hand. The Holy Spirit never descends upon prayerless people. He never fills them. He never empowers them. There is nothing whatsoever in common between the Spirit of God and people who do not pray. The Spirit dwells only in an atmosphere of prayer.

In doing God's work there is no substitute for praying. People of prayer cannot be replaced with other kinds of people. People of financial skill, people of education, people of worldly influence—none of these can possibly substitute for people of prayer. The life, the vigor, and the motive power of God's work is formed by praying people. A diseased heart is not a more fearful symptom of approaching death than non-praying people are of spiritual atrophy. *the washing away of the body organs*

The people to whom Jesus Christ committed the fortunes and destiny of His church were people of prayer. To no other kind of people has God ever committed Himself. The apostles were preeminently men of prayer. They gave themselves to prayer. They made praying their chief business. It was first in importance and first in results. God never has, and He never will, commit the weighty interests of His kingdom to people who do not make prayer a conspicuous and controlling factor in their lives. noticeable, obvious - Remarkable

People who do not pray never rise to any eminence of piety. People of piety are always people of prayer. People are never noted for the simplicity and strength of their faith unless they are preeminently people of prayer. Piety flourishes nowhere so rapidly and so profusely as in the prayer closet. The prayer closet is the garden of faith.

The apostles allowed no duty, however sacred, to so busy them that it infringed on their time and prevented them from making prayer the main thing. The Word of God was ministered with apostolic fidelity and zeal. It was spoken by people with apostolic commissions, people who had been baptized by the fiery tongues of Pentecost. The Word was pointless and powerless unless people were freshly clothed with power by continuous and mighty prayer. The seed of God's Word must be saturated in prayer to make it germinate. It grows more readily and anchors more deeply when it is soaked with prayer.

The apostles were praying people themselves. They were also teachers of prayer, and they trained their disciples in the school of prayer. They urged their disciples to pray, not only that they might attain to the loftiest eminence of faith, but that they might be the most powerful factors in advancing God's kingdom.

Jesus Christ is the divinely appointed leader of God's people, and no single thing in His life proves His eminent fitness for that office as much as His habit of prayer. Nothing is more food for thought than Christ's continual praying, and nothing is more conspicuous about Him than prayer. His campaigns were arranged, His victories gained, in the struggles and communion of His all-night praying. His praying rent the heavens. Moses and Elijah and the Transfiguration glory waited on His praying. His miracles and His teaching had their force from the same source. Gethsemane's praying crimsoned Calvary with serenity and glory. His prayer made the history and hastens the triumphs of His church. What an inspiration and command to pray is Christ's life! What a comment on its worth! How He shames our lives by His praying!

Like all those who have drawn God nearer to the world and lifted the world nearer to God, Jesus was a man of prayer. God made Him a leader and commander of His people. His leadership was one of prayer. A great leader He was, because He was great in prayer.

All great leaders for God have fashioned their leadership in the wrestlings of their prayer closets. Many great people have led and molded the church without being great in prayer, but they were great only in their plans, great for their opinions, great for their organization, great by natural gifts, great by genius or character. However, they were not great for God.

But Jesus Christ was a great leader for God. His was the great leadership of great praying. God was greatly in His leadership because prayer was greatly in it. We would do well to be taught by Him to pray, and to pray more and more.

Herein has been the secret of the people of prayer in the past history of the church: their hearts were after God, their desires were on Him, and their prayers were addressed to Him. They communed with Him, sought nothing of the world, sought great things of God, wrestled with Him, conquered all opposing forces, and opened up the channel of faith deep and wide between themselves and heaven. And all this was done by the use of prayer. Holy meditations, spiritual desires, heavenly longings— these swayed their intellects, enriched their emotions, and filled and enlarged their hearts. And all this was so because they were, first of all, people of prayer.

The people who have thus communed with God and have sought after Him with their whole hearts have always risen to consecrated eminence. In fact, no person has ever risen to this eminence without his flames of holy desire all dying to the world and all glowing for God and heaven. Nor have they ever risen to the heights of higher spiritual experiences unless prayer and the spirit of prayer have been conspicuous and controlling factors in their lives.

The entire consecration of many of God's children stands out distinctly like towering mountain peaks. Why is this? How did they ascend to these heights? What brought them so near to God? What made them so Christlike? The answer is easy—prayer. They prayed much, prayed long, and drank deeper and deeper still. They asked, they sought, and they knocked, until heaven opened its richest inner treasures of grace to them. Prayer was the Jacob's Ladder by which they scaled those holy and blessed heights and by which the angels of God came down and ministered to them.

The men and women of spiritual character and strength always valued prayer. They took time to be alone with God. Their praying was no hurried performance. They had many serious needs to be relieved and many weighty pleas to offer. They had to secure many great answers to prayer. They had to do much silent waiting before God, and much patient asking and asking over again. Prayer was the only channel through which the supply of their needs came, and it was the only way to utter pleas.

The only acceptable waiting before God of which they knew anything was prayer. They valued praying. It was more precious to them than all jewels, more excellent than any good, and more valued than the greatest good of earth. They esteemed it, valued it, and prized it. They pressed it to its farthest limits, tested its greatest results, and secured its most glorious heritage. To them prayer was the one great thing to be appreciated and used.

The apostles, above everything else, were praying people, and they left the stamp of their prayer example and teaching upon the early church. But the apostles are dead, and times and people have changed. They have no successors by official assignment or heirship. And we do not have a commission, in our times, to make other apostles. No, the apostles' successors are those who pray.

Unfortunately, the times are not prayerful times. God's cause just now is in dire need of praying leaders. Other things may be needed, but this is the crying demand of these times and the urgent, first need of the church.

This is the day of great wealth and wonderful material resources in the church. But, unfortunately, the abundance of material resources is a great enemy and a severe hindrance to strong spiritual forces. It is an invariable law that the presence of attractive and influential material resources creates a trust in them and, by the same inevitable law, creates distrust in the spiritual forces of the Gospel. They are two masters that cannot be served at the same time. (See Matthew 6:24.) For the degree to which the mind is fixed on one, it will be drawn away from the other. The days of great financial prosperity in the church have not been days of great religious prosperity. Wealthy people and praying people are not synonymous terms.

Paul, in the second chapter of his first epistle to Timothy, emphasized the need for people who pray. In his estimation, church leaders are to be conspicuous for their praying. Of necessity, prayer must shape their characters, and prayer must be one of their distinguishing characteristics. Prayer ought to be one of their most powerful elements, so much so that it cannot be hidden. Prayer ought to make church leaders notable. Character, official duty, reputation, and life—all should be shaped by prayer. The mighty forces of prayer lie in its praying leaders in a marked way. The standing obligation to pray rests in a special sense on church leaders. The church would be wise to discover this important truth and give prominence to it.

It can be written as a rule that God needs, first of all, leaders in the church who will put prayer first, people with whom prayer is habitual and characteristic, people who know the primacy of prayer. But, even more than having a habit of prayer, church leaders are to be filled to overflowing with prayer. Their lives should be made and molded by prayer; their hearts should be made up of prayer. These are the people—the only people—God can use in the furtherance of His kingdom and in the implanting of His message in the hearts of men.

infectious

Chapter Four

God's Need for People Who Pray

We do what He commands. We go where He wants us to go. We speak what He wants us to speak. His will is our law. His pleasure our joy. He is, today, seeking the lost, and He would have us seek with Him. He is shepherding the lambs, and He wants our cooperation. He is opening doors in heathen lands, and He wants our money and our prayers. —Anon.

As we proceed on the subject of prayer, we now declare that it demands prayer leadership to hold the church to God's aims and to prepare it for God's uses. Prayer leadership preserves the spirituality of the church, just as prayerless leaders make for unspiritual conditions. The church is not necessarily spiritual by the mere fact of its existence, nor by its vocation. It is not held to its sacred vocation by generation, nor by succession.

Like the new birth, it is "not of blood, nor of the will of the flesh, nor of the will of man, but of God" (John 1:13).

The church is not necessarily spiritual because it is concerned with and deals in spiritual values. It may hold its confirmations by the thousand, it may multiply its baptisms, and it may administer its sacraments innumerable times, and yet be as far from fulfilling its true mission as human conditions can make it.

This present world's general attitude retires prayer to insignificance and obscurity. By this attitude, salvation and eternal life are put in the background. It cannot be too often affirmed, therefore, that the principal need of the church is neither people of money nor people of intelligence, but people of prayer. Leaders in the realm of religious activity are to be judged by their praying habits, not by their money or social position. Those who are placed in the forefront of the church's business must be, first of all, people who know how to pray.

God does not conduct His work solely with people of education or wealth or business capacity. Neither can He carry on His work through people of large intellects or great culture, nor yet through people of great social eminence and influence. All these qualities can be useful in God's work, provided they are not regarded as being primary. People possessing only these qualities cannot lead in God's work nor control His cause. People of prayer, before anything else, are indispensable to the furtherance of the kingdom of God on earth. No other sort will fit in the scheme or do the deed. People, great and influential in other things but small in prayer, cannot do the work that God has set out for His church to do in this world.

People who represent God and who stand here in His stead, people who are to build up His kingdom in this world, must be, in an eminent sense, people of prayer. Whatever else they may have, whatever else they may lack, they must be people of prayer. Having everything else and lacking prayer, they will fail. Having prayer and lacking all else, they can succeed. Prayer must be the most conspicuous and the most potent factor in the character and conduct of people who undertake divine commission. God's business requires people who are versed in the business of praying.

It must be kept in mind that the praying to which the disciples of Christ are called by scriptural authority, is a valiant calling. The people God wants and on whom He depends, must work at prayer just as they work at their worldly callings. They must follow through in this business of praying, just as they do in their secular pursuits. Diligence, perseverance, heartiness, and courage must all be in it if it is to succeed.

Everything secured by gospel promise, defined by gospel measure, and represented by gospel treasure is in prayer. All heights are scaled by it, all doors are opened to it, all victories are gained through it, and all grace is obtained through it. Heaven has all its good and all its help for people who pray. How marked and strong is the command of Christ that sends people from the parade of public giving and public praying to the privacy of their prayer closets, where with shut doors and in encircling silence they are alone in prayer with God!

In all ages those who have carried out the divine will on earth have been people of prayer. The days of prayer are God's prosperous days. His heart, His oath, and His glory are committed to one proclamation: that every knee should bow to Him (Phil 2:10). The day of the Lord, in a preeminent sense, will be a day of universal prayer.

God's cause does not suffer because of lack of divine ability, but because of lack of prayer ability in man. God's action is just as much bound up in prayer today as it was when He said to Abimelech, "[Abraham] shall pray for thee, and thou shalt live" (Gen. 20:7). So it was when God said to Job's friends, "My servant Job shall pray for you: for him will I accept" (Job 42:8).

God's great plan for the redemption of mankind depends as much on prayer now as it did when the Father first decreed the plan. Prayer makes the plan of redemption prosper and succeed. For God gives an imperative, universal, and eternal condition: "Ask of me, and I shall give thee the heathen for thine inheritance, and the uttermost parts of the earth for thy possession" (Ps. 2:8).

In many places an alarming state of things has come to pass, in that many church members are not praying men and women. Many of those occupying prominent positions in church life are not praying people. It is greatly to be feared that much of the work of the church is being done by those who are perfect strangers to the prayer closet. No wonder the work does not succeed.

While it may be true that many in the church say prayers, it is equally true that their praying is of the stereotyped order. Their prayers may be charged with sentiment, but they are tame, timid, and without fire or force. This sort of praying is even done by some of the few people who attend prayer meetings. Those whose names are found looming large in our great churches are not people noted for their praying habits. Yet, the entire fabric of the work in which they are engaged has to, inevitably, depend on the adequacy of prayer. This lack of praying creates a crisis like that of a country admitting to an invading enemy that it cannot fight and knows nothing about weapons of war.

In all God's plans for human redemption, He purposes that people pray. We are to pray in every place—in the church, in the prayer closet, in the home. We are to pray on sacred days and on secular days. All things are dependent on the measure of people's praying.

Prayer is the mainspring of life. We pray as we live; we live as we pray. Life will never be finer than the quality of the prayer closet. The mercury of life will rise only by the warmth of the prayer closet. Persistent non-praying will eventually depress the temperature of life below zero.

If you were to measure and weigh the conditions of prayer, you would readily discover why more people do not pray. The conditions are so perfect, so blessed, that it is a rare character who can meet them. A heart full of love, a heart that holds even its enemies in loving contemplation and prayerful concern, a heart from which all bitterness, revenge, and envy are purged—how rare! Yet, this is the only condition of mind and heart in which a man can expect to be powerful in prayer.

There are certain conditions laid down for authentic praying. People are to pray, "lifting up holy hands" (1 Tim. 2:8), hands here being the symbol of life. Hands unsoiled by stains of evildoing are the emblem of a life unsoiled by sin. With a clean life, people are to come into the presence of God; thus they are to approach the throne of the Highest, where they can "obtain mercy, and find grace to help in time of need" (Heb. 4:16).

Here, then, is one reason why people do not pray. They are too worldly in heart and too secular in life to enter the prayer closet; and even though they enter there, they cannot offer the "effectual fervent prayer of a righteous man [which] availeth much" (James 5:16).

Again, hands are the symbols of supplication. Outstretched hands stand for an appeal for help. It is the silent yet eloquent attitude of a helpless soul standing before God, appealing for mercy and grace. Hands, too, are symbols of activity, power, and conduct. Hands outstretched to God in prayer must be "holy hands" (1 Tim. 2:8), unstained hands. The word "holy" here means undefiled, unspotted, untainted, and religiously observing every obligation.

How remote is all this from the character of sin-loving, worldly-minded, fleshly-disposed people, soiled by fleshly lusts, spotted by worldly indulgence, unholy in heart and conduct! "He who seeks equity must do equity" is the maxim of earthly courts. Even so, he who seeks God's good gifts must practice God's good deeds. This is the maxim of heavenly courts.

Prayer is sensitive, and it is always affected by the character and conduct of the one who prays. Water cannot rise above its own level, and a spotless prayer cannot flow from a spotted heart. Straight praying is never born of crooked conduct. The character of a person gives character to his supplication. The cowardly heart cannot do brave praying. Soiled people cannot make clean, pure supplications.

It is neither words, nor thoughts, nor ideas, nor feelings that shape praying, but it is character and conduct. People must walk in an upright fashion in order to be able to pray well. Bad character and unrighteous living break down praying until it becomes meaningless. Praying takes its tone and vigor from the life of the man or woman exercising it. When character and conduct are at a low ebb, praying can barely live, much less thrive.

The man of prayer, whether layman or preacher, is God's right-hand man. In the realm of spiritual affairs, he creates conditions, begins movements, and brings things to pass.

By the fact and condition of their creation and redemption, all people are under obligation to pray. Every person *can* pray, and every person *should* pray. But when it comes to the affairs of the kingdom, let it be said at once that a prayerless person in the church of God is like a paralyzed organ in the physical body. He is out of place in the communion of saints, out of harmony with God, and out of accord with His purposes for mankind. A prayerless person handicaps the vigor and life of the whole system, just as a demoralized soldier is a menace to his army in the day of battle. The absence of prayer lessens the life-giving current of the soul, cripples faith, sets aside holy living, and shuts out heaven.

The Holy Scriptures draw a sharp line between praying saints and non-praying people. The following was written about John Fletcher of Madeley—one of the praying saints:

> He was far more abundant in his public labors than the greater part of his companions in the holy ministry. Yet these bore but little proportion to those internal exercises of prayer and supplication to which he was wholly given up in private, which were almost uninterruptedly maintained from hour to hour. He lived in the spirit of prayer, and whatever employment in which he was engaged, this spirit of prayer was constantly manifested through them all.

Chapter Five

Prayerless Christians

If there was ever a time when Peter, James and John needed to remain awake, it was in Gethsemane. If James had persisted in keeping awake, it might have saved him from being decapitated a few years later. If Peter had stirred himself to really intercede for himself and others, he would not have denied his Christ that night in the palace of Caiaphas. —H. W. Hodge

There is great need in this day for Christians in the business world to infuse their mundane affairs with the spirit of prayer. There is a great army of successful businesspeople in Christ's church, and it is high time they attended to this matter. We need to put God into business. In other words, we need to put the realization and restraint of His presence and His fear into all the secularities of life.

We need the atmosphere of the prayer closet to pervade our places of business. The sanctity of prayer is needed to fill our workplaces. We need the spirit of Sunday carried over to Monday and continued until Saturday. But this cannot be done by prayerless people; we need people of prayer. We need businesspeople to go about their concerns with the same reverence and responsibility with which they enter the prayer closet. We need people who are devoid of greed and who carry God with them, with all their hearts, into the secular affairs of life.

Worldlings imagine prayer to be too impotent a thing to battle with business methods and worldly practices. Against such a misleading doctrine Paul sets the whole commands of God, the loyalty to Jesus Christ, the claims of pious character, and the demands of the salvation of the world. We must pray, and we must put strength and heart into our praying. Prayer is part of the primary business of life, and God has called His people to it first of all.

Praying people are God's agents on earth, the representatives of the government of heaven, called to a specific task on the earth. While it is true that the Holy Spirit and the angels are agents of God in carrying forward the redemption of the human race, yet among them there must be praying people. For such people God has great use. He can make much of them, and in the past He has done wonderful things through them. These are God's instruments in carrying out His great purposes on the earth. They are God's messengers, watchmen, shepherds, and workmen, who need not be ashamed. Fully equipped for the great work to which they are appointed, they honor God and bless the world.

Above all things, Christian men and women must, primarily, be leaders in prayer. No matter how conspicuous they may be in other activities, they fail if they are not conspicuous in prayer. They must give their brains and hearts to prayer. People who shape the program of Christ's church, who map out its line of activity, should, themselves, be shaped by prayer. People controlling the finances, thought, and action of the church should all be people of prayer.

In order for God's work to progress to completion, there are two basic principles: God's ability to give and people's ability to ask. Failure in either one would be fatal to the success of God's work on earth. God's inability to do or to give would put an end to redemption. People's failure to pray would, just as surely, set a limit on the plan. But, God's ability to do and to give has never failed and *cannot* fail, but people's ability to ask can fail and often does.

Therefore, the slow progress that is being made toward the realization of a world won for Christ lies entirely with people's limited asking. There is need for the entire church of God to get busy praying. The church upon its knees would bring heaven upon the earth.

The wonderful ability of God to do for us was expressed by Paul in one of his most comprehensive statements: "And God is able to make all grace abound toward you; that ye, always having all sufficiency in all things, may abound to every good work" (2 Cor. 9:8).

Study that remarkable statement—"God is able to make all grace abound." That is, He is able to give such sufficiency that we may abound—overflow—to every good work. Why are we not more fully overflowing? The answer is lack of prayer ability. "[We] have not, because [we] ask not" (James 4:2). We are feeble, weak, and impoverished because of our failure to pray. God is restrained in doing because we are restrained by our failure to pray. All failures in securing heaven are traceable to lack of prayer or misdirected prayer.

Prayer must be broad in its scope; it must plead for others. Intercession for others is the hallmark of all true prayer. When prayer is confined to self and to the sphere of one's personal needs, it dies by reason of its littleness, narrowness, and selfishness. Prayer must be broad and unselfish, or it will perish. Prayer is the soul of a person stirred to plead with God for others. In addition to being interested in the eternal interests of one's own soul, it must, in its very nature, be concerned for the spiritual and eternal welfare of others. A man is most able to pray for himself when he has compassion and concern for others.

In the second chapter of 1 Timothy, apostle Paul spoke to those who occupied tions of influence and places of authorit urged them with singular and specific emphasis to give themselves to prayer. "I will therefore that men pray every where" (1 Tim. 2:8). This is the high calling of the men of the church, and no other calling is so engaging, so engrossing, and so valuable that we can afford to relieve Christian men from the all-important vocation of secret prayer. Nothing whatsoever can take the place of prayer. Nothing whatsoever can atone for the neglect of praying. This is of supreme importance, and it should be given first priority.

No person is so high in position or in grace to be exempt from the obligation to pray. No person is too big to pray, no matter who he is or what office he holds. The king on his throne is as much obligated to pray as the peasant in his cottage. No one is so high and exalted in this world, or so lowly and obscure, that he is excused from praying. Everyone's help is needed in doing the work of God, and the prayer of each praying person helps to swell the whole. Those who are leaders in place, in gifts, and in authority are to be chiefs in prayer.

Civil and church leaders shape the affairs of this world. Therefore, civil and church leaders themselves need to be shaped personally in spirit, in heart, in conduct, in truth, and in righteousness, by the prayers of God's people. This is in direct line with Paul's words:

> *I exhort therefore, that, first of all, supplications, prayers, intercessions, and giving of thanks, be made for all men; For kings, and for all that are in authority.*   *(1 Tim. 2:1–2)*

It is a sad day for righteousness when church politics, instead of holy praying, shapes the administration of the church and elevates people to place and power.

Why must we pray for all people? Because God wills the salvation of all people. God's children on earth must link their prayers to God's will. Prayer is meant to carry out the will of God. God's will is that all people would be saved. His heart is set on this one thing. Our prayers must be the creation and exponent of God's will. We are to grasp humanity in our praying as God grasps humanity in His love, His interest, and His plans to redeem them. Our sympathies, prayers, wrestlings, and ardent desires must run parallel with the will of God and be broad, generous, worldwide, and godlike. A Christian must in all things, first of all, be conformed to the will of God, but nowhere should this royal devotion be more evident than in the salvation of the human race. This high partnership with God, as His agents on earth, is to have its fullest, richest, and most effective exercise in prayer for all people.

Believers are to pray for all people, especially for rulers in church and state, "that we may lead a quiet and peaceable life in all godliness and honesty" (1 Tim. 2:2). Peace on the outside and peace on the inside. Praying calms disturbing forces, allays tormenting fears, and brings conflict to an end. Prayer tends to do away with turmoil. Even if there are external conflicts, it is well to have deep peace within the citadel of the soul. "That we may lead a quiet and peaceable life." Prayer brings inner calm and furnishes outward tranquillity. If there were praying rulers and praying subjects worldwide, they would allay turbulent forces, make wars to cease, and cause peace to reign.

Believers must pray for all people so that we may lead lives "in all godliness and honesty," that is, with godliness and seriousness. Godliness means to be like God. It means to be godly, to have godlikeness, to have the image of God stamped on the inner nature, and to show the same likeness in our conduct and character. Almighty God is the very highest model, and to be like Him is to possess the highest character. Prayer molds us into the image of God. At the same time it tends to mold others into the same image in proportion to our praying for them.

Prayer means to be like God. To be godlike is to love Christ and love God, to be one with the Father and the Son in spirit, character, and conduct. Prayer means to stay with God until you are like Him. Prayer makes a person godly, and it puts within him "the mind of Christ" (1 Cor. 2:16), the mind of humility, self-surrender, service, pity, and prayer. If we really pray, we will become more like God, or else we will quit praying.

"Men [are to] pray every where"—in the prayer closet, in the prayer meeting, around the family altar—and they are to do it, "lifting up holy hands, without wrath and doubting" (1 Tim. 2:8). Here is not only the obligation laid upon people to pray, but instructions on how they should pray. People must pray "without wrath." In other words, people must pray without bitterness against their neighbors or fellow believers, without the stubbornness of a strong will, without hard feelings, without an evil desire or emotion kindled by fires in the carnal nature. Praying is not to be done by these questionable things or in company with such evil feelings, but "without" them, aloof and entirely separate from them.

This is the sort of praying we are called upon to do. It is the sort that God hears and the kind that prevails with God and accomplishes things. Such prayers in Christians' hands become divine agencies in God's hands for carrying on God's gracious purposes and executing His designs in redemption.

Prayer has a higher origin than man's nature. This is true whether we mean man's nature as separate from the angelic nature, or man's carnal nature unrenewed and unchanged. Prayer does not originate in the realm of the carnal mind. Such a nature is entirely foreign to prayer simply because "the carnal mind is enmity against God" (Rom. 8:7).

It is by the new spirit that we pray, the new spirit sweetened by the sugar of heaven, perfumed with the fragrance of the upper world, and invigorated by a breath from the crystal sea. The new spirit is native to the skies, panting after the heavenly things, and inspired by the breath of God. The new spirit produces praying from which all the old juices of the carnal, unregenerate nature have been expelled. It is praying in which the fire of God has created the flame that has consumed worldly lusts. At the same time, the juices of the Spirit have been injected into the soul. Praying that is by the new spirit is entirely divorced from wrath.

People are also to pray "without...doubting" (1 Tim. 2:8). The Revised Version puts it, "without...disputing." Praying people must have faith in God and belief in God's Word without question. There must be no doubting or disputing in the mind. There must be no opinions, no hesitancy, no questioning, no reasoning, no intellectual quibbling, no rebellion, but a strict, steadfast loyalty of spirit to God, a life of loyalty in heart and intellect to God's Word.

God is closely related to people who have a living, transforming faith in Jesus Christ. These are God's children. A father loves his children, supplies their needs, hears their cries, and answers their requests. A child believes his father, loves him, trusts in him, and asks him for what he needs, believing without doubting that his father will hear his requests. God answers the prayers of His children. Their troubles concern Him, and their prayers awaken

Him. Their voices are sweet to Him. He loves to hear them pray, and He is never happier than to answer their prayers.

Prayer is intended for God's ear. It is not people but God who hears and answers prayer. Prayer covers the whole range of human need. Hence, "in every thing by prayer and supplication with thanksgiving let your requests be made known unto God" (Phil. 4:6). Prayer includes the entire range of God's ability. "Is any thing too hard for the LORD?" (Gen. 18:14). Prayer does not apply to one favored segment of man's need, but it reaches to and embraces the entire circle of his needs, simply because God is the God of the whole man. God has pledged Himself to supply the needs of the whole man: physical, intellectual, and spiritual. "But my God shall supply all your need according to his riches in glory by Christ Jesus" (Phil. 4:19). Prayer is the child of grace, and grace is for the whole man and for every one of the children of men.

(Lan-gwəd)

Languid - Weak, sluggish in
Character or disposition, Listless
slow

avowed - to declare openly

promulgate - to make known
or put into force by open declaration

propagate - to reproduce or
Cause to reproduce, biologically
Multiply, to cause to spread

Peter to be released from prison

Chapter Six

Praying for Others

Ep 5:19-20
Paul ask the churches to pray for him

Our Redeemer was in the Garden of Gethse-mane. His hour was come. He felt as if He would be strengthened somewhat, if He had two or three disciples near Him. His three chosen disciples were within a stone's throw of the scene of His agony; but they were all asleep that the Scripture might be fulfilled—"I have trodden the winepress alone; and of the people there was none with me" (Isa. 63:3). The eight, in the distance, were good and true disciples; but they were only ordinary men, or men with a commonplace call.

—Alexander Whyte

No insistence in the Bible is more pressing than the command it lays upon people to pray. No exhortation contained therein is more hearty, more solemn, or more stirring. No principle is more strongly stressed than "men ought always to pray, and not to faint" (Luke 18:1).

75

In view of this command, it is pertinent to ask if the majority of Christians are praying men and women. Is prayer a fixed course in the churches? In the Sunday school, the home, and the colleges, do we have any graduates in the school of prayer? Is the church producing those who have diplomas from the great university of prayer? This is what God requires, what He commands. It is those who possess such qualifications that He must have to accomplish His purposes and to carry out the work of His kingdom on earth.

And it is earnest praying that needs to be done. Languid praying, without heart or strength, with neither fire nor tenacity, defeats its own avowed purpose. The prophet of past times lamented that in a day that needed strenuous praying, there was no one who stirred up himself to take hold of God (Isa. 64:7). Christ charges us "not to faint" (Luke 18:1) in our praying. Laxity and indifference are great hindrances to prayer, both to the practice of praying and the process of receiving. It requires a brave, strong, fearless, and insistent spirit to engage in successful prayer.

Trying to pray for too many things also interferes with effectiveness. Offering too many petitions breaks unity and breeds neglect. Prayers should be specific and urgent. Too many words, like too much width, causes

shallowness and sandbars. A single objective
that absorbs the whole being and inflames the
entire person is the properly constraining force
in prayer.

It is easy to see how prayer was a decreed
factor in the dispensations before the coming
of Jesus, how their leaders had to be men of
prayer, and how God's mightiest revelations of
Himself were revelations made through
prayer. It is also easy to see how Jesus Christ,
in His personal ministry and in His relationship to God, was great and constant in prayer.
His labors and dispensation overflowed with
fullness in proportion to His prayers. The possibilities of His praying were unlimited, as
were the possibilities of His ministry. The necessity of His praying was equaled only by the
constancy with which He practiced it during
His earthly life.

The dispensation of the Holy Spirit is a
dispensation of prayer in a preeminent sense.
Here prayer has an essential and vital role.
Without depreciating the possibilities and ne-
cessities of prayer in all the preceding dispensations of God in the world, it must be declared
that it is in this latter dispensation that the
exercises and demands of prayer are given
their greatest authority. Furthermore,
prayer's possibilities are rendered unlimited,
and its necessity unavoidable.

In these days we have sore need of a generation of praying people, a band of men and women through whom God can bring His greatest movements more fully into the world. The Lord our God is not restricted within Himself, but He is restricted in us by reason of our little faith and weak praying. A breed of Christians is greatly needed who will seek tirelessly after God, who will give Him no rest, day and night, until He hearkens to their cries. The times demand people who are all athirst for God's glory, who are unselfish in their desires, who are quenchless for God, who seek Him late and early, and who will give themselves no rest until "the whole earth be filled with his glory" (Ps. 72:19).

Men and women are needed whose prayers will give to the world the utmost power of God, whose prayers will make His promises blossom with rich and full results. God is waiting to hear us, and He challenges us to pray that He might work. He is asking us today, as He asked His ancient Israel, to "prove [Him] now herewith" (Mal. 3:10). Behind God's Word is God Himself. We read in Isaiah 45:11,

Thus saith the LORD, the Holy One of Israel, and his Maker, Ask me of things to come concerning my sons, and concerning the work of my hands command ye me.

It is as though God places Himself in the hands and at the disposal of His people who pray, and indeed He does.

The dominant element of all praying is faith that is conspicuous, cardinal, and emphatic. Without such faith it is impossible to please God (Heb. 11:6) and equally impossible to pray.

There is a current perception of spiritual duties that tends to separate the pulpit and the pew. The perception is that the pulpit should bear the entire burden of spiritual concerns, while the pew should be concerned only with secular and worldly duties. Such a view needs drastic correction. God's cause, obligations, efforts, and successes lie with equal pressure on pulpit and pew.

The person in the pew is not taxed with the burden of prayer as he ought to be, and as he must be, before any new visitation of power can come to the church. The church will never be wholly for God until the pews are filled with praying people. The church cannot be what God wants it to be until the members that are leaders in business, politics, law, and society are also leaders in prayer.

God began His early movements in the world with people of prayer. Abraham, a leader of God's cause, was preeminently a praying man. God chose Abraham to be the father of the race that became His chosen people in the world for hundreds of years. This was the race to whom God committed His oracles and from whom sprang the promised Messiah.

When we consider Abraham's conduct and character, we readily see how prayer ruled and swayed this great leader of God's people. "Abraham planted a grove in Beersheba, and called there on the name of the LORD, the everlasting God" (Gen. 21:33). It is an outstanding fact that wherever he pitched his tent and camped for a season with his household, there he erected an altar of sacrifice and of prayer. His was a personal and a family religion, in which prayer was a prominent and abiding factor.

Prayer is the medium of divine revelation. It is through prayer that God reveals Himself to the spiritual soul today, just as in the Old Testament days He made His revelations to the people who prayed. God shows Himself to the person who prays.

"God is with thee in all that thou doest" (Gen. 21:22). This was the clear conviction of Abraham's peers, and they gladly would have made a covenant with him. It was the commonly held belief that Abraham was not only a man of prayer, but a man whose prayers God would answer. This is the summary and secret of divine rule in the church. In all ages God has ruled the church by prayerful people. When prayer fails, the divine rulership fails.

As we have seen, Abraham, the father of the faithful, was a prince and a priest in prayer. He had remarkable influence with God. God held back His vengeance while Abraham prayed. His mercy was suspended and conditioned on Abraham's praying. His visitations of wrath were removed by the praying of this ruler in Israel. The movements of God were influenced by the prayers of Abraham, the friend of God. Abraham's righteous prayerfulness permitted him to share in the secrets of God's counsels, while the knowledge of these secrets lengthened and intensified his praying. With Abraham the altar of sacrifice was close to the altar of prayer. With him the altar of prayer sanctified the altar of sacrifice. To Abimelech God said, "[Abraham] is a prophet, and he shall pray for thee, and thou shalt live" (Gen. 20:7).

Christian people must pray for others. On one occasion Samuel said to the people, "Moreover as for me, God forbid that I should sin against the LORD in ceasing to pray for you" (1 Sam. 12:23). Fortunately, these sinful Israelites, who had rejected God and desired a human king, had a man of prayer.

One way to increase personal grace is to pray for others. Intercessory prayer is a means of grace to those who exercise it. It is in the paths of intercessory prayer that we enter the richest fields of spiritual growth and gather priceless riches. To pray for others is of divine appointment, and it represents the highest form of Christian service. It dispels selfishness

People must pray, and people must be prayed for. The Christian must pray for all things, of course, but prayers for people are infinitely more important, just as people are infinitely more important than things. Also, prayers for people are far more important than prayers for things because people more deeply involve God's will and the work of Jesus Christ. People are to be cared for, sympathized with, and prayed for, because sympathy, pity, compassion, and care accompany and precede prayer for people.

All this makes praying a real business, not child's play, not a secondary affair, not a trivial matter, but a serious business. The people who have made a success of praying have made a business of praying. It is a process demanding the time, thought, energy, and hearts of mankind. Prayer is business for time, business for eternity. It is our business to pray, transcending all other business and taking precedence over all other vocations, professions, or occupations. Our praying concerns not only ourselves, but all people and their greatest interests, and even the salvation of their immortal souls. Praying is a business that takes hold of eternity and the things beyond the grave. It is a business that involves earth and heaven. All worlds are touched by prayer, and all worlds are influenced by prayer. It has to do with God and people, angels and devils.

Jesus was preeminently a leader in prayer, and His praying is an incentive to pray. How prominently prayer stands out in His life! The leading events of His earthly career are distinctly marked by prayer. The wonderful experience and glory of the Transfiguration was preceded by prayer, and it was the result of the praying of our Lord. (See Luke 9:28–35.) We do not know what words He used as He prayed, nor do we know what He prayed for. But I believe it was night, and long into its hours the Master prayed. It was while He prayed that the darkness fled and His form was lit with unearthly splendor. Moses and Elijah came to yield to Him not only the palm of law and prophecy, but the palm of praying.

None other prayed as Jesus did, nor did any have such a glorious manifestation of the divine presence. None other heard so clearly the revealing voice of the Father: "This is my beloved Son: hear him" (Luke 9:35). Oh, to be with Christ in the school of prayer; then we would be happy disciples indeed!

How many of us have failed to come to this glorious Mount of Transfiguration because we were unacquainted with the transfiguring power of prayer! It is the going apart to pray and the long, intense seasons of prayer that make the face shine, transfigure the character, and make even dull, earthly garments glisten with heavenly splendor. But more than this: it is real praying that makes eternal things real, close, and tangible, and real praying brings the glorified visitors and the heavenly visions. Transfigured lives would not be so rare if there were more of this transfigured praying, and these heavenly visits would not be so few.

How difficult it seems to be for the church to understand that the whole scheme of redemption depends on people of prayer. The work of our Lord, while here on the earth, as well as the work of the apostle Paul, was to develop, by teaching and example, people of prayer, to whom the future of the church would be committed. How strange that instead of learning this simple and all-important lesson, the modern church has largely overlooked it. We need to turn afresh to that wondrous leader of spiritual Israel, our Lord Jesus Christ, who by example and precept instructs us to pray. And we need to turn to the apostle Paul, who, by virtue of his praying habits and prayer lessons, is a model to God's people in every age and place.

prayer to the Lord of the harvest

Chapter Seven

Preachers and Prayer

Of course, the preacher is above all others distinguished as a man of prayer. He prays as an ordinary Christian, else he were a hypocrite. He prays more than ordinary Christians, else he were disqualified for the office he has undertaken. If you as ministers are not very prayerful, you are to be pitied. If you become lax in sacred devotion, not only will you need to be pitied but your people also, and the day cometh in which you will be ashamed and confounded. Our seasons of fastings and prayer at the Tabernacle have been high days indeed; never has heaven's gate stood wider; never have our hearts been nearer the central glory. —Charles H. Spurgeon

Preachers are God's leaders. They are divinely called to their holy office and high purpose and, primarily, are responsible for the condition of the church. Just as Moses was called of God to lead Israel out of

Egypt through the wilderness into the Promised Land, so also God calls His ministers to lead His spiritual Israel through this world to the heavenly land. They are divinely commissioned to leadership, and they are, by precept and example, to teach God's people what God would have them be. Paul's counsel to the young preacher Timothy is this:

> *Let no man despise thy youth; but be thou an example of the believers, in word, in conversation, in charity, in spirit, in faith, in purity.*   *(1 Tim. 4:12)*

God's ministers shape the church's character and give tone and direction to its life. In Revelation chapters two and three, the prefacing sentence in the letters to each of the seven churches in Asia reads, "Unto the angel of the church." This seems to indicate that the angel—the minister—was in the same state of mind and condition of life as the membership, and, moreover, the minister was largely responsible for the spiritual condition of the church. The angel in each case was the preacher, teacher, or leader.

The first Christians knew this full well and felt this responsibility. In their helplessness, which they consciously felt, they cried out, "And who is sufficient for these things?"

(2 Cor. 2:16), for the tremendous responsibility pressed upon their hearts and heads. The only reply to such a question was, "God only" (Mark 2:7). So, they were compelled by necessity to look beyond themselves for help and to throw themselves on prayer to secure God. More and more, as they prayed, they felt their responsibility; and more and more, by prayer they got God's help. They realized that their sufficiency was in God.

Prayer belongs in a very high and important sense to the ministry. It takes vigor and elevation of character to administer the prayer office. Praying prophets have frequently been at a premium in the history of God's people. In every age the demand has been for leaders in Israel who pray. God's watchmen must always and everywhere be people of prayer.

It ought to be no surprise for ministers to be often found on their knees seeking divine help for the responsibilities of their call. These are the true prophets of the Lord, and they stand as mouthpieces of God to a generation of wicked and worldly-minded men and women. Praying preachers are the boldest, the truest, and the swiftest ministers of God. They mount up highest and are nearest to Him who has called them. They advance more rapidly, and in Christian living they are most like God.

The Weapon of Prayer

In reading the Gospels, we cannot help being impressed by the supreme effort made by our Lord to rightly instruct the twelve apostles. He instructed them in all the things that would prepare them for the tremendous tasks ahead of them. His consideration was for the church, that it would have people, holy in life and in heart, who would know full well the origin of their strength and power in the work of the ministry. A large part of Christ's teaching was addressed to these chosen apostles, and the training of the Twelve occupied much of His thought and time. In all that training, prayer was laid down as a basic principle.

We find the same thing to be true in the life and work of the apostle Paul. Though he edified the churches to whom he ministered and wrote, it was his purpose to instruct and prepare ministers to whom the interests of God's people would be committed. Paul wrote two epistles to Timothy, who was a young preacher, and one to Titus, who was also a young minister. It appears that Paul's design was to give each of them needed instruction to rightly do the work of the ministry to which they had been called by the Spirit of God. Underlying these instructions was the foundation stone of prayer. Unless they were men of prayer, by no means would they be able to "show [themselves] approved unto God, [workmen] that need[ed] not to be ashamed, rightly dividing the word of truth" (2 Tim. 2:15).

The highest welfare of the church of God on earth depends largely on the ministry, and so God has always been jealous of His watchmen—His preachers. His concern has been for the character of the people who minister at His altars in holy things. They must be people who lean on Him, who look to Him, and who continually seek Him for wisdom, help, and power to effectively do the work of the ministry. So, He has designed people of prayer for the holy office, and He has relied on them successively to perform the tasks He has assigned them.

God's great works are to be done as Christ did them; they are to be done, indeed, with increased power received from the ascended and exalted Christ. These works are to be done by prayer. People must do God's work in God's way and to God's glory, and prayer is necessary for its successful accomplishment.

The thing far above all other things in the equipment of the preacher is prayer. Before everything else he must be a person who makes a specialty of prayer. A prayerless preacher is a misnomer. He has either missed his calling, or he has grievously failed God, who called him into the ministry.

God wants people who are not dullards, who "study to show [themselves] approved" (2

Misnomer- a wrong name or designation

Tim. 2:15). Preaching the Word is essential, social qualities are not to be underestimated, and education is good. But under and above all else, prayer must be the main plank in the platform of the one who goes forth to preach the unsearchable riches of Christ to a lost and hungry world.

The one weak spot in our church institutions lies just here. Prayer is not regarded as being the primary factor in church life and activity; and other things, good in their places, are made primary. This should not be. First things need to be put first, and the first thing in the equipment of a minister is prayer.

Our Lord is the pattern for all preachers, and with Him prayer was the law of life. By it He lived. It was the inspiration of His toil, the source of His strength, and the spring of His joy. With our Lord prayer was no sentimental episode, nor a pleasing prelude, nor an interlude, nor an afterthought, nor a form. For Jesus, prayer was exacting, all-absorbing, and paramount. To Him it was the call of a sweet duty, the satisfying of a restless yearning, the preparation for heavy responsibilities, and the meeting of a vigorous need.

This being so, the disciple must be as his Lord, the servant as his Master. As the Lord Himself was, so also His disciples must be.

paramount →superior to all other supreme

Our Lord Jesus Christ chose His twelve apostles only after He had spent a night in praying, and we may rest assured that He sets the same high value on those He calls into His ministry today.

No feeble or secondary place was given to prayer in the ministry of Jesus. It comes first—emphatic, conspicuous, and controlling. Having prayerful habits, having a prayerful spirit, given to long, solitary communion with God, Jesus was above all else a man of prayer. The crux of His earthly history, in New Testament terminology, is condensed to a single statement, found in Hebrews 5:7:

> *Who in the days of his flesh, when he had offered up prayers and supplications with strong crying and tears unto him that was able to save him from death, and was heard in that he feared.*

Let Jesus' ministers be like their Lord and Master, whose they are and whom they serve (Acts 27:23). Let Him be their pattern, their example, their leader, and their teacher. In some places much reference is made to "following Christ," but it is confined to the following of Him in modes and ordinances, as if salvation were wrapped up in the specific way of doing a thing. "The path of prayer Thyself hath trod" is the path along which we are to follow Him; no other path will do.

Jesus was given as a leader to the people of God, and never has any leader more exemplified the worth and necessity of prayer. Even though he was equal in glory with the Father, and anointed and sent on His special mission by the Holy Spirit, Jesus still prayed. His incarnate birth, His high commission, His royal anointing—all these were His, but they did not relieve Him from the exacting claims of prayer. Rather, they tended to impose these claims upon Him with greater authority. He did not ask to be excused from the burden of prayer; He gladly accepted it, acknowledged its claims, and voluntarily subjected Himself to its demands.

Not only was His leadership preeminent, but His praying was preeminent. Had it not been, His leadership would have been neither preeminent nor divine. If, in true leadership, prayer had been dispensable, then certainly Jesus could have dispensed with it. But He did not, nor can any of His followers who desire effectiveness in Christian activity do other than follow their Lord.

While Jesus Christ was personally under the law of prayer and while His parables and miracles were exponents of prayer, He focused on teaching His disciples the specific art of praying. He said little or nothing about how to preach or what to preach. But, He spent both His strength and His time in teaching people how to speak to God, how to commune with Him, and how to be with Him. He knew very well that he who has learned the craft of talking to God will be well versed in talking to people.

Turning aside for a moment, we observe that prayer was the secret of the wonderful success of the early Methodist preachers, who were far from being learned people. But with all their limitations, they were people of prayer, and they did great things for God.

The ability to talk to people is measured by the ability with which a preacher can talk to God for people. He who does not plow in his prayer closet will never reap in his pulpit.

We must always emphasize that Jesus Christ trained His disciples to pray. This is the real meaning of the saying, "the training of the Twelve." We must remember that Christ taught the world's preachers more about praying than He did about preaching. Prayer was the great factor in the spreading of His Gospel. Prayer preserved and made effective all other factors. He did not discount preaching when He stressed praying, but rather He taught that preaching is utterly dependent on prayer.

"The Christian's trade is praying," declared Martin Luther. Every Jewish boy had to learn a trade. Jesus Christ learned two: the trade of a carpenter and the trade of praying. The one trade served earthly uses; the other served His divine and higher purposes. Jewish custom committed Jesus as a boy to the trade of a carpenter; the law of God bound Him to praying from His earliest years and remained with Him to the end.

Christ is the Christian's example, and every Christian must imitate Him. Every preacher must be like his Lord and Master and must learn the trade of praying. He who learns well the trade of praying, masters the secret of the Christian art; and he becomes a skilled workman in God's workshop, one who does not need to be ashamed, a worker together with his Lord and Master.

"Pray without ceasing" (1 Thess. 5:17) is the trumpet call to the preachers of our time. If the preachers will clothe their thoughts with the atmosphere of prayer, if they will prepare their sermons on their knees, a gracious outpouring of God's Spirit will come upon the earth.

The one indispensable qualification for preaching is the gift of the Holy Spirit, and it was for the bestowal of this indispensable gift that the disciples were charged to stay in

Jerusalem. Receiving this gift is absolutely necessary if ministry is to be successful. This is why the first disciples were commanded to stay in Jerusalem until they received it. This is why they sought the gift with urgent and earnest prayerfulness. They obeyed their Lord's command to stay in that city until they were clothed with "power from on high" (Luke 24:49). Immediately after He had left them for heaven, they sought to secure it by continued and earnest prayer. "These all with one accord continued stedfastly in prayer, with the women, and Mary the Mother of Jesus, and with his brethren" (Acts 1:14 RV).

John refers to this same thing in his first epistle. He says, "Ye have an unction from the Holy One" (1 John 2:20). It is this divine unction that preachers of the present day should sincerely desire and pray for, remaining unsatisfied until the blessed gift is richly bestowed.

Another allusion to this same important procedure was made by our Lord shortly after His resurrection, when He said to His disciples, "But ye shall receive power, after that the Holy Ghost is come upon you" (Acts 1:8). At the same time Jesus directed the attention of His disciples to the statement of John the Baptist concerning the Spirit. John had said, "I indeed baptize you with water; but...he shall baptize you with the Holy Ghost and with fire"

(Luke 3:16). This is identical to the "power from on high" (Luke 24:49) for which Jesus had commanded them to stay in the city of Jerusalem. Alluding to John the Baptist's words, Jesus said, "For John truly baptized with water; but ye shall be baptized with the Holy Ghost not many days hence" (Acts 1:5). Peter at a later date said of our Lord, "God anointed [Him] with the Holy Ghost and with power" (Acts 10:38).

These are the divine statements to preachers of that day about the mission and ministry of the Holy Spirit, and the same divine statements apply with equal force to the preachers of today. God's ideal minister is a God-called, divinely anointed, Spirit-touched man. He is separated unto God's work; set apart from secularities and questionable affairs; baptized from above; marked, sealed, and owned by the Spirit; and devoted to his Master and His ministry. These are the divinely appointed requisites for a preacher of the Word; without them he is inadequate and inevitably unfruitful.

Today, there is no scarcity of preachers who deliver eloquent sermons on the need and nature of revival, who advance elaborate plans for the spread of the kingdom of God. But the praying preachers are rare. The greatest benefactor this age can have is a person who will bring the preachers, the church, and the people back to the practice of real praying. The reformer needed just now is the praying reformer. The leader Israel requires is one who, with clarion voice, will call the ministry back to their knees. Clarion —brilliantly clear

There is considerable talk in the air about revival. However, we need the vision to see that the revival we need, and the only one worth having, is the one that is born of the Holy Spirit. This kind of revival brings deep conviction for sin and regeneration for those who seek God's face. Such a revival comes at the end of a season of real praying. It is utter folly to discuss or expect a revival without the Holy Spirit operating in His distinctive office, and this is conditioned on much earnest praying. Such a revival will begin in pulpit and pew alike; it will be promoted by both preacher and layman working in harmony with God.

The heart is the vocabulary of prayer, the life is the best commentary on prayer, and the outward conduct is the fullest expression of prayer. Prayer builds the character; prayer perfects the life. And this the ministry needs to learn as thoroughly as the laymen. There is but one rule for both.

The general body of Christ's disciples was averse to prayer, having little taste for it and having little harmony with Him in the deep things of prayer and its mightier struggles. Therefore, the Master had to select a circle of three more apt scholars—Peter, James, and John—who had more relish for this divine work. He took them aside that they might learn the lesson of prayer. These men were nearer to Jesus, more like Him, and more helpful to Him because they were more prayerful.

Blessed, indeed, are those disciples whom Jesus Christ, in this day, calls into a more intimate fellowship with Himself, and who, readily responding to the call, are found much on their knees before Him. Distressing, indeed, is the condition of the Christians who, in their hearts, are averse to exercising the ministry of prayer.

All the great eras of our Lord, historical and spiritual, were made or fashioned by His praying. So, also, His plans and great achievements were born in prayer and filled with the spirit thereof. As was the Master, so also must His servant be; as his Lord did in the great eras of His life, so should the disciple do when faced by important crises. "To your knees, O Israel!" should be the clarion call to the ministry of this generation.

The highest form of religious life is attained by prayer. The richest revelations of God—Father, Son, and Spirit—are made, not to the learned, the great, or the noble of earth, but to people of prayer. "For ye see your calling, brethren, how that not many wise men after the flesh, not many mighty, not many noble, are called" (1 Cor. 1:26). God makes known His deep things and reveals the higher things of His character to the lowly, inquiring, praying ones. And, again, it must be said that this is as true of preachers as of laymen. It is the spiritual person who prays, and to praying ones God makes His revelations through the Holy Spirit.

Praying preachers have always brought the greater glory to God and have moved His Gospel onward with its greatest, speediest rate and power. A non-praying preacher and a non-praying church might flourish outwardly and advance in many aspects. Both preacher and church might even become synonyms for success. But unless success rests on a foundation of prayer, it will eventually crumble into death and decay.

"Ye have not, because ye ask not" (James 4:2) is the solution of all spiritual weakness both in the personal life and in the pulpit. Either that or it is, "Ye ask, and receive not, because ye ask amiss" (James 4:3). Real praying lies at the foundation of all the real success that the ministry has in the things of God. The stability, readiness, and energy with which God's kingdom is established in this world are dependent on prayer. God has made it so, and therefore God is eager for people to pray. He is especially concerned that His chosen ministers should be people of prayer, and so He gives this wonderful statement in order to encourage His ministers to pray:

> *And I say unto you, Ask, and it shall be given you; seek, and ye shall find; knock, and it shall be opened unto you. For every one that asketh receiveth; and he that seeketh findeth; and to him that knocketh it shall be opened.*
>
> *(Luke 11:9–10)*

Thus, both command and direct promise give accent to His concern that they should pray. Pause and think on these familiar words: "Ask, and it shall be given you." That verse itself would seem to be enough to set us all, laymen and preachers, to praying. These words are so direct, simple, and unlimited. They open all the treasures of heaven to us, simply by asking for them.

We should study the prayers of Paul, who was primarily a preacher to the Gentiles; otherwise, we can have only a feeble view of the great necessity for prayer and of how much it is worth in the life and work of a minister. Furthermore, we will have only a very limited view of the possibilities of the Gospel to enrich, strengthen, and perfect Christian character, as well as equip preachers for their high and holy task. Oh, when will we learn the simple yet all-important lesson that the one great thing needed in the life of a preacher to help him in his personal life, to keep his soul alive to God, and to give efficacy to the Word he preaches, is real, constant prayer!

Paul, with prayer uppermost in his mind, assured the Colossians that "Epaphras...[is] always labouring fervently for you in prayers, that ye may stand perfect and complete in all the will of God" (Col. 4:12). He prayed that they may come to this high state of grace, "complete in all the will of God." So, prayer was the force that was to bring them to that elevated, vigorous, and stable state of heart.

This is in line with Paul's teaching to the Ephesians: "And he gave some...pastors and teachers; for the perfecting of the saints, for the work of the ministry, for the edifying of the body of Christ" (Eph. 4:11–12). These verses evidently affirm that the whole work of the ministry is not merely to induce sinners to repent, but it is also the "perfecting of the saints." So, Epaphras labored fervently in prayers for this thing. Certainly, he was himself a praying man, for he earnestly prayed for these early Christians.

The apostles put forth their efforts in order that Christians should honor God by the purity and consistency of their outward lives. Christians were to reproduce the character of Jesus Christ. They were to perfect His image in themselves, incorporate His character, and reflect His behavior in all their attitudes and conduct. They were to be "imitators of God, as beloved children" (Eph. 5:1 RV), to be holy as He was holy (1 Pet. 1:16). Thus, even laymen were to preach by their conduct and character, just as the ministry preached with their mouths.

To elevate the followers of Christ to these exalted heights of Christian experience, the apostles were in every way true in the ministry of God's Word—in the ministry of prayer, in holy zeal, in burning exhortation, in rebuke and reproof. Added to all these, sanctifying all these, invigorating all these, and making all these beneficial, they centered on and exercised constantly the force of mightiest praying. "Night and day praying exceedingly" means praying superabundantly, beyond measure, and with intense earnestness.

Night and day praying exceedingly that we might see your face, and might perfect that which is lacking in your faith. Now God himself and our Father, and our Lord Jesus Christ, direct our way unto you. And the Lord make you to increase and abound in love one toward another, and toward all men, even as we do toward you: To the end he may stablish your hearts unblameable in holiness before God, even our Father, at the coming of our Lord Jesus Christ with all his saints. (1 Thess. 3:10–13)

It was after this fashion that these apostles, the first preachers in the early church, labored in prayer. And only those who labor after the same fashion are the true successors of these apostles. This is the true, scriptural "apostolical succession": the succession of simple faith, earnest desire for holiness of heart and life, and zealous praying. These are the things today that make the ministry strong, faithful, and effective and make "a workman that needeth not to be ashamed, rightly dividing the word of truth" (2 Tim. 2:15).

Jesus Christ, God's leader and commander of His people, lived and suffered under this law of prayer. All His personal conquests in His life on earth were won by obedience to this law. And the conquests won by His representatives since He ascended to heaven, were gained only when this condition of prayer was heartily and fully met. Christ was under this one prayer condition. His apostles were under the same prayer condition. His saints are under it, and even His angels are under it. By every token, therefore, preachers are under the same prayer law. Not for one moment are they relieved or excused from obedience to the law of prayer. It is their very life, the source of their power, the secret of their religious experience and communion with God.

Christ could do nothing without prayer. Christ could do all things by prayer. The apostles were helpless without prayer. They were absolutely dependent on it for success in defeating their spiritual foes. Like Christ, they could do all things by prayer.

Chapter Eight

Prayerlessness
in the Pulpit

*Henry Martyn laments that "want of private
devotional reading and shortness of prayer
through incessant sermon-making had produced
much strangeness between God and his soul." He
judges that he had dedicated too much time to
public ministrations and too little to private
communion with God. He was much impressed
with the need of setting apart times for fasting
and devoting times to solemn prayer. Resulting
from this he records, "Was assisted this morning
to pray for two hours." —E. M. Bounds*

All God's saints came to their sainthood
by the way of prayer. The saints could
do nothing without prayer. We can go
further and say that the angels in heaven can
do nothing without prayer but can do all
things by praying. These messengers of the

Highest are largely dependent on the prayers of the saints for the sphere and power of their usefulness. Prayer opens avenues for angelic usefulness and creates missions for them on the earth. And, as it is with all the apostles, saints, and angels in heaven, so it is with preachers. The preachers, also called the angels of the churches, can do nothing without prayer, which opens doors of usefulness and gives power and point to their words.

How can a preacher preach effectively, make impressions on hearts and minds, and have fruits in his ministry, if he does not get his message firsthand from God? How can he deliver a fitting message without having his faith quickened, his vision cleared, and his heart warmed by his communion with God?

It would be well for all of us, in connection with this thought, to read again Isaiah's vision. As he waited and confessed and prayed before the throne, the angel touched his lips with a live coal from God's altar.

> *Then flew one of the seraphims unto me, having a live coal in his hand, which he had taken with the tongs from off the altar: And he laid it upon my mouth, and said, Lo, this hath touched thy lips; and thine iniquity is taken away, and thy sin purged.* (Isa. 6:6–7)

Oh, the need there is for present-day preachers to have their lips touched with a live coal from the altar of God! This fire is brought to the mouths of those prophets who are of a prayerful spirit and who wait in the secret place for the appointed angel to bring the living flame. Preachers of Isaiah's character received visits from an angel who brought live coals to touch their lips. Prayer always brings the living flame in order to unloose tongues, to open "door[s] of utterance" (Col. 4:3), and to open great and effective doors of doing good. This, above all else, is the great need of the prophets of God.

As far as the abiding interests of religion are concerned, a pulpit without a prayer closet will always be a barren thing. Blessed is the preacher whose pulpit and prayer closet are close to each other, and who goes from the one into the other.

To consecrate no place to prayer is to make a beggarly showing, not only in praying, but in holy living; for secret prayer and holy living are so closely joined that they can never be separated. A preacher or a Christian may live a decent, religious life without secret prayer, but decency and holiness are two widely different things. And holiness is attained only by secret prayer.

A preacher may preach in an official, entertaining, and learned way without prayer, but there is a great distance between this kind of preaching and the sowing of God's precious seed.

We cannot declare too often or too strongly that prayer, involving all of its elements, is the one prime condition of the success of Christ's kingdom and that all else is secondary and incidental. Only prayerful preachers, prayerful men, and prayerful women can advance this Gospel with aggressive power. Only they can put conquering forces into it. Preachers may be sent out by the thousand, and their equipment may be ever so complete; but unless they are skilled in the trade of prayer, trained to its martial and exhaustive exercise, their going will be lacking in power and effectiveness. Moreover, unless the men and women who are behind these preachers, who furnish their equipment, are men and women whose prayers are serious labor, their efforts will be vain and fruitless.

Prayer should be the inseparable accompaniment of all missionary effort, and prayer must be the one piece of equipment of the missionaries as they go out to their fields of labor and begin their delicate and responsible tasks. Prayer and missions go hand in hand. A prayerless missionary is a failure before he goes out, while he is out, and when he returns to his native land. A prayerless board of missions, too, needs to learn the necessity of prayer.

Added to all the missionary speeches, the money raised for missions, and the dozens being sent out to needy fields, is prayer. Missions has its root in prayer, and missions must have prayer in all of its plans. Prayer must precede, go with, and follow all of its missionaries and laborers.

Prayer enthrones God as sovereign and elevates Jesus Christ to sit with Him. If Christian preachers had used the power of prayer to its fullest, long before this "the kingdoms of this world [would have] become the kingdoms of our Lord, and of his Christ" (Rev. 11:15).

Huge difficulties face the church in its great work on earth, and almost superhuman and complex obstacles stand in the way of evangelizing the world. In the face of all this, God encourages us by His strongest promises: "Call unto me, and I will answer thee, and show thee great and mighty things, which thou knowest not" (Jer. 33:3). God commits Himself to answer the specific prayer, but He does not stop there. The revelations of God to him who is of a prayerful spirit go far beyond the limits of the actual praying.

He says, "Ask me of things to come concerning my sons, and concerning the work of my hands command ye me" (Isa. 45:11). Think over that remarkable pledge of God to those who pray: "Command ye me." He actually places Himself at the command of praying preachers and a praying church. This is a sufficient answer to all doubts, fears, and unbelief. This is a wonderful inspiration to do God's work in God's way—by prayer.

Furthermore, as if to fortify even more the faith of His ministry and of His church, to protect against any temptation to doubt or be discouraged, He declares by the mouth of the great Apostle to the Gentiles, "[He] is able to do exceeding abundantly above all that we ask or think" (Eph. 3:20).

It is unquestionably taught that, in going forward with their God-appointed tasks, preachers can command God in their prayers. To pray is to command His ability, His presence, and His power. "Certainly I will be with thee" (Exod. 3:12) is the reply to every sincere, inquiring minister of God. All of God's called workers in the ministry are privileged to stretch their prayers into regions where neither words nor thoughts can go. They are permitted to expect from Him beyond their praying. For their praying, they can expect God Himself and then, in addition, "great and mighty things, which thou knowest not" (Jer. 33:3).

Real, live, heart praying by the power of the Spirit—praying that is direct, specific, ardent, and simple—is the kind of praying that legitimately belongs to the pulpit. This is the kind demanded just now of the preachers who stand in the pulpit. There is no school in which to learn to pray in public except the prayer closet. Preachers who have learned to pray in the prayer closet have mastered the secret of pulpit praying. It is but a short step from secret praying to effective, live, pulpit praying. Good pulpit praying follows good secret praying. An empty prayer closet makes for cold, spiritless, formal praying in the pulpit.

Oh, preacher, study how to pray, not by studying the forms of prayer, but by attending the school of prayer on your knees before God. Here is where we learn not only how to pray before God, but also how to pray in the presence of people. He who has learned the way to the prayer closet has discovered the way to pray in the pulpit.

How easily we become businesslike and mechanical in the most sacred undertakings! Henry Martyn learned the lesson so hard to learn, that the cultivation and perfection of personal righteousness is the prime factor in the preacher's success. Likewise, he that learns another lesson so hard to learn—that live, spiritual, effective pulpit praying is the outgrowth of regular secret praying—has learned his lesson well. Moreover, his work as a preacher will depend on his praying.

The great need of the hour is for good pray-ers in the pulpit as well as good preachers. Just as live, spiritual preaching is the kind that impresses and moves men, so live, spiritual praying in the pulpit moves and impresses God. The preacher is called not only to preach well, but also to pray well. Not that he is called to pray after the fashion of the Pharisees, who love to stand in public and pray so that they may be seen and heard of men (Matt. 6:5). The right sort of pulpit praying is far removed from pharisaical praying, as far as light is from darkness, as far as heat is from cold, as far as life is from death.

Preaching is the very loftiest work possible for a person to do. And praying goes hand in hand with preaching. It is a mighty, lofty work. Preaching is a life-giving work, sowing the seeds of eternal life. Oh, may we do it well, do it after God's order, and do it successfully! May we do it divinely well, so that when the end comes, the solemn close of earthly probation, we may hear from the Great Judge of all the earth, "Well done, good and faithful servant...enter thou into the joy of thy lord" (Matt. 25:23).

When we consider this great question of preaching, we are led to exclaim, "With what reverence, simplicity, and sincerity it ought to be done!" What truth in the inward parts is

praying is not great formal swelling words but sincereness of the heart, cry

demanded in order that it be done acceptably *and seeking* to God and with profit to men! How real, true, *god* and loyal those who practice it must be! How *for* great the need to pray as Christ prayed, with strong cryings, tears, and godly fear!

use Oh, may preachers do the real thing of preaching, with no sham, with no mere form of words, with no dull, cold, professional discourses. May they give themselves to prayerful preaching and prayerful praying! Preaching that gives life is born of praying that gives life. Preaching and praying always go together, like Siamese twins, and can never be separated without death to one or the other, or death to both.

This is not the time for kid-glove methods or sugar-coated preaching. This is no time for playing the gentleman as a preacher, nor for putting on the garb of the scholar in the pulpit. We want to disciple all nations, destroy idolatry, crush the defiant forces of Islam, and destroy the tremendous forces of evil now opposing the kingdom of God. Brave people, true people, praying people—afraid of nothing but God—are the kind needed just now. There will be no smiting the forces of evil that now hold the world in bondage, no lifting of the degraded hordes of paganism to light and eternal life, by any but praying people. All others are merely playing at religion, make-believe soldiers with no armor or ammunition, who are absolutely helpless in the face of a wicked and opposing world. None but soldiers and bond servants of Jesus Christ can possibly do this tremendous work.

"Endure hardness, as a good soldier of Jesus Christ" (2 Tim. 2:3), cries the great apostle. This is no time to think of self, to consult with dignity, to confer with flesh and blood (Gal. 1:16), to think of ease, or to shrink from hardship, grief, and loss. This is the time for toil, suffering, and self-denial. We must lose all for Christ in order to gain all for Christ (Phil. 3:8). People are needed in the pulpit, as well as in the pew, who are bold enough to take up and firm enough to sustain the consecrated cross. Here is the sort of preachers God wants, and this sort is born of much praying. For no prayerless preacher is sufficient for these things. Only praying preachers can meet the demand and be equal to the emergency.

The Gospel of Jesus has neither relish nor life in it when spoken by prayerless lips or handled by prayerless hands. Without prayer the doctrines of Christ degenerate into dead orthodoxy. Preaching them without the aid of the Spirit of God, who comes into the preacher's messages only by prayer, is nothing more than mere lecturing with no life, no grip, and no force. It amounts to nothing more than *preacher who to see their ministry flourishing and overflow with peace... thoughts must be men and women of prayer*

pure rationalism or sickly sentimentalism.
"But we will give ourselves continually to
prayer, and to the ministry of the word" (Acts
6:4) was the settled and declared purpose of
the apostolic ministry. The kingdom of God
waits on prayer, and prayer puts wings on and
power into the Gospel. By prayer it moves forward with conquering force and rapid advance.

If prayer is left out, the preacher rises to
no higher level than the lecturer, the politi-
cian, or the secular teacher. That which distinguishes him from all other public speakers is
the fact of prayer. Because prayer deals with
God, the preacher has God with him, while
other speakers do not need God with them to
make their public messages effective. The
preacher above everything else is a spiritual
person, a person of the Spirit, and he deals
with spiritual things. And this implies that he
has to do with God in his pulpit work in a high
and holy sense. This can be said of no other
public speaker. So, prayer must of necessity go
with the preacher and his preaching. Pure in-
tellectuality is the only qualification for other
public speakers. Spirituality, which is born of
prayer, belongs to the preacher.

In the Sermon on the Mount, Jesus
Christ often speaks of prayer. It stands out
prominently in His words on that occasion.
The lesson of prayer that He taught was one

of hallowing God's name, of advancing God's kingdom. We are to long for the coming of the kingdom of God. It is to be longed for, and it must be first in our communication with God. God's will must have its royal way in the hearts and wills of those who pray. The point of urgency is made by our Lord that people are to pray in earnest—by asking, seeking, knocking—in order to hallow God's name, bring His will to pass, and forward His kingdom.

And let it be kept in mind that while this prayer lesson has to do with all people, it has a special application to the ministry; for it was the twelve would-be preachers who made the request, "Lord, teach us to pray, as John also taught his disciples" (Luke 11:1). So, primarily, Jesus' reply was spoken first to twelve men just starting their work as ministers. Jesus was talking, as Luke records it, to preachers. He also speaks to the preachers of this day. How He pressed these twelve men into the ministry of prayer! Present-day ministers need the same lesson to be taught to them, and they need the same urgency pressing them to make prayer their habit of life.

Regardless of all a preacher may claim for himself, or how many good things may be put down to his credit, a prayerless preacher will never master God's truth, which he is called upon to declare with all fidelity and plainness of speech. Blind and blinding will he be if he lives a prayerless life. A prayerless ministry cannot know God's truth and, not knowing it, cannot teach it to ignorant people. He who teaches us the path of prayer must first of all walk in the same path. A preacher cannot teach what he does not know. The preacher who is a stranger to prayer will be a blind leader of the blind. Prayer opens the preacher's eyes, and prayer keeps them open to the evil of sin, the peril of sin, and the penalty of sin. A blind leader leading the blind will be the vocation of the one who is prayerless in his own life.

The best and the greatest offering that the church and the ministry can make to God is an offering of prayer. If the preachers of the twentieth century will learn well the lesson of prayer and use it fully in all its exhaustless effectiveness, the Millennium will come to its noon before the century closes.

The Bible preacher prays. He is filled with the Holy Spirit, filled with God's Word, and filled with faith. He has faith in God; he has faith in God's only begotten Son, his personal Savior; and he has implicit faith in God's Word. He cannot do otherwise than pray. He cannot be other than a person of prayer. The breath of his life and the throb of his heart are

- prayer. The Bible preacher lives by prayer, loves by prayer, and preaches by prayer. His bended knees in the place of secret prayer advertise what kind of a preacher he is.

Preachers may lose faith in God, lose faith in Jesus Christ as their personal and present Savior, become devoid of the peace of God, and let the joy of salvation go out of their hearts, yet be unconscious of it. How needful for the preacher to be continually examining himself and to be checking his religious state and his personal relationship with God!

The preachers, like the philosophers of old, may defer to a system and then earnestly contend for it even after they have lost all faith in its great facts. Preachers may preach in the pulpit with hearts of unbelief; they may minister at the altars of the church while being alien to the most sacred and vital principles of the Gospel.

It is a comparatively easy task for preachers to become so absorbed in the material and external affairs of the church that they lose sight of their own souls, forget the necessity of life-giving prayer, and lose the inward sweetness of the Christian experience.

Prayer makes much of preaching, and we must make much of prayer. The character of our praying will determine the character of our preaching. Serious praying will give serious weight to preaching. Prayer makes preaching strong, gives it unction, and makes it stick. In every beneficial ministry, prayer has been a serious business.

It cannot be said with too much emphasis: the preacher must be preeminently a person of prayer. He must learn to pray. He must have such an estimate of prayer and its great worth that he feels he cannot afford to omit it from his list of private duties. His heart must be attuned to prayer, while he himself touches the highest note of prayer. Only in the school of prayer can the heart learn to preach. No gifts, no learning, no brainpower can atone for the failure to pray. No earnestness, no diligence, no study, no amount of social service will supply its lack. Talking to people for God may be a great thing, and it may be very commendable. But talking to God for people is far more valuable and commendable.

The power of Bible preaching does not lie solely in superlative devotion to God's Word and jealous passion for God's truth. Both of these are essential, valuable, and helpful. But, above these things, a preacher must have a sense of the divine presence. He must be conscious of the divine power of God's Spirit on him and in him. For the great work of preaching, he must have an anointing, an empowering, a sealing of the Holy Spirit, making him speak God's words and giving him the energy of God's right hand. Such a preacher can say,

> *Thy words were found, and I did eat them; and thy word was unto me the joy and rejoicing of mine heart: for I am called by thy name, O LORD God of hosts.* (Jer. 15:16)

Chapter Nine

Equipped by Prayer

Go back! Back to that upper room; back to your knees; back to searching of heart and habit, thought and life; back to pleading, praying, waiting, till the Spirit of the Lord floods the soul with light, and you are "endued with power from on high" (Luke 24:49). Then go forth in the power of Pentecost, and the Christ-life shall be lived, and the works of Christ shall be done. You shall open blind eyes, cleanse foul hearts, break men's fetters, and save men's souls. In the power of the indwelling Spirit, miracles become the commonplace of daily living. —Samuel Chadwick

Almost the last words uttered by our Lord before His ascension were those addressed to the eleven disciples. They were words which really were spoken to, and directly had to do with, preachers. These words indicated very clearly the power these people needed in order to preach the Gospel, beginning at Jerusalem. These vital words of Jesus are recorded in Luke 24:49: "And, behold, I send the promise of my Father upon you: but tarry ye in the city of Jerusalem, until ye be endued with power from on high."

Two things are very clearly set forth in these urgent directions. The first thing is the power of the Holy Spirit for which they must wait. This was to be received after their conversion. This power was an indispensable requisite, equipping them for the great task set before them.

The second thing is the truth that the "promise of my Father," this "power from on high," would come to them after they had waited in earnest, continuous prayer. A reference to Acts 1:14 will reveal that these same men, with the women, "continued with one accord in prayer and supplication," and so continued until the Day of Pentecost when the power from on high descended upon them.

This power from on high is as important to those early preachers as it is to present-day preachers. This power was not the force of a mighty intellect, holding in its grasp great truths, flooding them with light, and forming them into verbal shapeliness and beauty. Nor was it the acquisition of great learning. Nor was it the result of a speech, faultless and complete by the rules of rhetoric. It was none of these things. This spiritual power was not held then, nor is it held now, in the keeping of any earthly sources of power. Human forces are essentially different in source and character; they are not a result of this power from on high. On the contrary, the transmission of such power is directly from God.

Power from on high is a bestowal, in rich measure, of the force and energy that pertains only to God. The Master transmits this power to His messenger only in answer to the longing, wrestling attitude of his soul. The messenger is conscious of his own impotency and seeks the omnipotence of the Lord he serves. He seeks God's power in order that he may more fully understand the given Word and preach it to his fellowmen.

The power from on high may be found in combination with all sources of human power, but it is not to be confused with them, is not dependent on them, and must never be superseded by them. Whatever human gift, talent, or force a preacher may possess, it is not to be made paramount, or even conspicuous. It must be hidden, lost, and overshadowed by this power from on high. The forces of intellect and culture may all be present, but without this inward, heaven-given power, all spiritual effort is vain and unsuccessful.

Even when lacking the other equipment but having this power from on high, a preacher cannot help but succeed. It is the one essential, all-important, vital force that a messenger of God must possess to give wings to his message, to put life into his preaching, and to enable him to speak the Word with power and acceptance.

I need to clarify something here. Distinctions need to be kept in mind. We must think clearly about the meaning of our terms. Power from on high means the "unction from the Holy One" (1 John 2:20) resting on and abiding in the preacher. This is not so much a power that bears witness to a person being the child of God as it is a preparation for delivering the Word to others. Also, unction must be distinguished from pathos. (Pathos causes an emotional response in the hearer; unction causes a spiritual response.) Pathos may exist in a sermon in which unction is entirely absent. So also unction may be present and pathos absent. Both may exist together, but they are not to be confused, nor should they be made to appear to be the same thing. Pathos promotes emotion, tender feeling, sometimes tears. Quite often it results when a sad story is told or when the tender side is appealed to. But pathos is neither the direct nor the indirect result of the Holy Spirit resting upon the preacher as he preaches.

However, unction is. Here we are given the evidence of the workings of an undefinable agency in the preacher; these workings result directly from the presence of this power from on high. Unction is deep, conscious, life-giving, and carrying. It gives power and point to the preached Word. It is the element in a sermon that arouses, stirs, convicts, and moves the souls of sinners and saints. This is what the preacher requires, the great equipment for which he should wait and pray. This "unction from the Holy One" (1 John 2:20) delivers from dryness, saves from superficiality, and gives authority to preaching. It is the one quality that distinguishes the preacher of the Gospel from other people who speak in public; it is that which makes a sermon unique, unlike any other public address.

Prayer is the language of a person burdened with a sense of need. It is the voice of the beggar, conscious of his poverty, asking of another the things he needs. It is not only the language of lack, but of *felt* lack, of lack consciously realized. "Blessed are the poor in spirit" (Matt. 5:3) means not only that poverty of spirit brings the blessing, but also that poverty of spirit is realized, known, and acknowledged. Prayer is the language of those who need something—something which they, themselves, cannot supply but which God has promised them—and so they ask.

In the end, poor praying and prayerlessness amount to the same thing; for poor praying proceeds from a lack of the sense of need, while prayerlessness has its origin in the same soil. Not to pray is to declare there is nothing needed and to admit there is no realization of a need. This is what magnifies the sin of prayerlessness. It represents an attempt at instituting an independence of God, a self-sufficient ruling of God out of the life. It is a declaration made to God that we do not need Him and hence do not pray to Him.

This is the state in which the Holy Spirit, in His messages to the seven churches in Asia, found the Laodicean church. The "Laodicean state" has come to stand for one in which God is ruled out, expelled from the life, put out of the pulpit. The entire condemnation of this church is summed up in one expression: "Because thou sayest, I...have need of nothing" (Rev. 3:17). This is the most alarming state into which a person, a church, or a preacher can come. Trusting in its riches, in its social position, in its outward and material things, the church at Laodicea omitted God, leaving Him out of their church plans and church work. They declared, by their acts and by their omission of prayer, "I...have need of nothing."

No wonder the self-satisfied declaration brought forth its sentence of punishment: "Because thou art lukewarm, and neither cold nor hot, I will spue thee out of my mouth" (Rev. 3:16). The idea conveyed is that such a backslidden state of heart is as repulsive to God as spoiled food is to the human stomach. As the stomach expels that which is objectionable, so almighty God threatened to vomit out of His mouth these people who were in a religious condition so repulsive to Him.

All of it was traceable to a prayerless state of heart, for no one can read this word of the Spirit to the Laodicean church and not see that the very core of their sin was prayerlessness. How could a church given to prayer openly and arrogantly declare, "I...have need of nothing," in the face of the Spirit's assertion that it needed everything: "Thou...knowest not that thou art wretched, and miserable, and poor, and blind, and naked" (Rev. 3:17)?

In addition to their sins of self-sufficiency and independence of God, the Laodiceans were spiritually blind. Oh, what dullness of sight, what blindness of soul! These people were prayerless, and they did not know the import of such prayerlessness. They lacked everything that makes up spiritual life and force and self-denying piety, and they vainly supposed themselves to need nothing but material wealth. Thus, they tried to make temporal possessions a substitute for spiritual wealth. They left God entirely out of their activities. They relied on human and material resources to do the work that is possible only to divine and supernatural intervention through prayer.

Nor let it be forgotten that this letter (in common with the other six letters) was primarily addressed to the preacher in charge of the church. All this strengthens the impression that the "angel of the church" (Rev. 3:14) himself was in this lukewarm state. He himself was living a prayerless life, relying on things other than God, practically saying, "I...have need of nothing" (Rev. 3:17). For these words are the natural expression of the spirit of him who does not pray, who does not care for God, and who does not feel the need of Him in his life and work and preaching. Furthermore, the words of the Spirit seem to indicate that the "angel of the church" at Laodicea was indirectly responsible for this sad condition into which the Laodicean church had fallen.

May not this sort of a church be found in modern times? Could we not discover some preachers who fall under a condemnation similar to that of the "angel of the church" at Laodicea?

Preachers of the present age excel those of the past in many, possibly in all, human

elements of success. They are well abreast of
the age in learning, research, and intellectual
vigor. But these things neither ensure power
from on high nor guarantee a righteous life or
a thriving religious experience. These purely
human gifts do not bring with them an insight
into the deep things of God, a strong faith in
the Scriptures, or an intense loyalty to God's
divine revelation.

The presence of these earthly talents, even
in the most commanding and impressive form
and richest measure, do not in the least abate
the necessity for the added endowment of the
Holy Spirit. Herein lies the great danger men-
acing the pulpit of today. All around us we see
a tendency to substitute human gifts and
worldly attainments for that supernatural, inward power that comes from heaven in answer
to earnest prayer.

In many instances modern preaching
seems to fail in the very thing that should dis-
tinguish true preaching, that is essential to its
being, and that alone can make it a powerfully
aggressive agency. It lacks, in short, power
from on high, which alone can make it a living
thing. It fails to become the channel through
which God's saving power can appeal to people's consciences and hearts.

Quite often, modern preaching fails to
reach people because it does not have a potent

influence that disturbs people in their sleep of security and awakens them to a sense of need and of peril. There is a growing need of an appeal that will quicken and arouse the conscience from its ignoble stupor, an appeal that will give the conscience a sense of wrongdoing and a corresponding sense of repentance. There is need of a message that searches into the secret places of a man's being, dividing, as it were, the joints and the marrow and laying bare the mysterious depths before himself and his God (Heb. 4:12).

Much of our present-day preaching lacks power to infuse new blood into the heart and veins of faith, to arm with courage and skill for the battle against the powers of darkness, and to get a victory over the forces of the world. Such high and noble ends can never be accomplished by human qualifications. Nor can these great results be secured by a pulpit clothed only with the human elements of power, however gracious, comfortable, and helpful they may be.

The Holy Spirit is needed. He alone can equip the ministry for its difficult and responsible work in and out of the pulpit. Oh, that the present-day ministry may come to see that its one great need is an outpouring of power from on high. May they see that this one need can be secured only by the use of God's appointed means of grace—the ministry of prayer.

Prayer is needed by the preacher in order that his personal relationship with God may be maintained, for there is no difference between him and any other person as far as his personal salvation is concerned. This he must work out "with fear and trembling" (Phil. 2:12) just as all other people must do. Thus, prayer is of vast importance to the preacher in order that he may possess a growing religious experience. Prayer enables him to live such a life that his character and conduct will back up his preaching and give force to his message.

A person must have prayer in preparing to preach, for no minister can preach effectively without prayer. He also has use for prayer in praying for others. Paul was a notable example of a preacher who constantly prayed for those to whom he ministered.

But we come, now, to another sphere of prayer: people praying for the preacher. "Brethren, pray for us" (1 Thess. 5:25). This is the cry that Paul set in motion, and this has been the cry of spiritually-minded preachers—those who know God and who know the value of prayer—in all succeeding ages. No amount of success or failure must abate the cry. No amount of refinement and no abundance of talents must cause that cry to cease. The learned preacher, as well as the unlearned, has equal need to call out to the people he serves, "Withal praying also for us" (Col. 4:3).

Such a cry voices the felt need of a preacher's heart, a preacher who feels the need for his people to be in harmony with him. Such a cry is the expression of the inner soul of a preacher who feels his insufficiency for the tremendous responsibilities of the pulpit. He realizes his weakness and his need of the divine unction, and therefore he throws himself upon the prayers of his congregation and calls out to them, "Praying always with all prayer and supplication in the Spirit...and for me, that utterance may be given unto me" (Eph. 6:18–19). It is the cry of the preacher who deeply feels in his heart that he must have this prayer made specifically for him so that he may do his work in God's own way.

When this request to a people to pray for the preacher is cold, formal, and official, it freezes instead of bearing fruit. To be ignorant of the necessity for the cry, is to be ignorant of the sources of spiritual success. To fail to stress the cry, and to fail to have responses to it, is to sap the sources of spiritual life. Preachers must sound out the cry to the church of God. Saints everywhere and of every kind and of every faith speedily respond and pray for the preacher. The imperative need of the work demands it. "Pray for us" (1 Thess. 5:25) is the natural cry of the hearts of God's called ministers, the faithful preachers of the Word.

Saintly praying in the early church helped apostolic preaching mightily, and it rescued apostolic believers from many severe troubles. It can do the same thing today. It can open doors for apostolic labors; it can open doors for apostolic lips to utter bravely and truly the gospel message. Apostolic movements wait their ordering from prayer, and avenues long closed are opened to apostolic entrance by and through the power of prayer. The messenger receives his message and is schooled as to how to carry and deliver the message by prayer. The forerunner of the Gospel, and that which prepares the way, is prayer, not only by the praying of the messenger himself, but by the praying of the church of God.

Writing along this line in his second epistle to the Thessalonians, Paul was general at first in his request and said, "Brethren, pray for us." Then he became more minute and particular:

> *Finally, brethren, pray for us, that the word of the Lord may have free course, and be glorified, even as it is with you: And that we may be delivered from*

> *unreasonable and wicked men: for all*
> *men have not faith.* (2 Thess. 3:1–2)

In the Revised Version, "have free course" is replaced by the word "run." "The word" means doctrine, and the idea conveyed is that this doctrine of the Gospel is running a race. In other words, it is being rapidly propagated. This verse is an exhortation to exert one's self, to strive hard, to expend strength. Thus, the prayer for the spread of the Gospel gives the same energy to the Word of the Lord as the greatest output of strength gives success to the racer. Prayer in the pew gives the preached Word energy, attainment, and success. Preaching without the backing of mighty praying is as limp and worthless as can be imagined. Prayerlessness in the pew is a serious hindrance to the running of the Word of the Lord.

The preaching of God's Word fails to run and be glorified from many causes. The difficulty may lie with the preacher himself, if his outward conduct is out of harmony with the rule of the Scriptures and his own profession. He must live the Word and not just preach the Word; his life must be in harmony with his sermon. The preacher's spirit and behavior out of the pulpit must run parallel with the Word of the Lord spoken in the pulpit. Otherwise, a man is an obstacle to the success of his own message.

Again, the Word of the Lord may fail to run, may be seriously encumbered and crippled, by the inconsistent lives of those who are the hearers of it. Bad living in the pew will seriously cripple the Word of the Lord as it attempts to run on its appointed course. Unrighteous lives among the laity heavily weigh down the Word of the Lord and hamper the work of the ministry.

Yet, prayer will remove this unrighteous living that seriously handicaps the preached Word. It will tend to do this in a direct way or in an indirect way. For just as you set laymen to praying, for the preacher or even for themselves, it awakens conscience, stirs the heart, and tends to correct evil ways and promote good living. No one will pray for long and continue in sin. Prayer breaks up bad living, and bad living breaks down prayer. Praying goes into bankruptcy when a person goes into sin. Obeying the cry of the preacher, "Brethren, pray for us" (2 Thess. 3:1), gets people to do that which will induce right living in them; it tends to break them away from sin.

For these reasons it is worth a great deal to get the laity to pray for the ministry. Prayer helps the preacher, is an aid to the sermon, assists the hearer, and promotes right living in the pew. Prayer also moves the one who prays for the preacher and for the Word of the Lord. It moves him to use all his influence to remove any hindrance to the Word which he may see and which lies in his power to remove.

But prayer reaches the preacher directly. God hears the praying of a church for its minister. Prayer for the preached Word is a direct aid to it. Prayer for the preacher gives wings, as well as feet, to the Gospel. Prayer makes the Word of the Lord go forward strongly and rapidly. It takes the shackles off of the message and gives it a chance to run straight to the hearts of sinners and saints alike. It opens the way, clears the track, and furnishes a free course.

The failure of many a preacher may be found just here. He is hampered, hindered, and even crippled by a prayerless church. Non-praying church workers stand in the way of the Word preached; they become veritable stumbling blocks in the way of the Word, definitely preventing its reaching the hearts of the unsaved.

Unbelief and prayerlessness go together. It is written of our Lord in Matthew's gospel that when He entered into His own country, "he did not many mighty works there because of their unbelief" (Matt. 13:58). Mark puts it a little differently but gives the same idea:

*And he could there do no mighty work,
save that he laid his hands upon a few
sick folk, and healed them. And he mar-
velled because of their unbelief.*

(Mark 6:5–6)

Unquestionably, the unbelief of that people hindered our Lord in His gracious work
and tied His hands. And, if that is true, we
would not be stretching the Scriptures to say
that the unbelief and prayerlessness of a
church can tie the hands of its preacher and
prevent him from doing many great works in
the salvation of souls and in edifying saints.

Prayerlessness, therefore, as it concerns
the preacher, is a very serious matter. If it ex-
ists in the preacher himself, then he ties his
own hands and makes his own preaching of the
Word ineffective and void. If prayerless people
are found in the pew, then they hurt the
preacher, rob him of an invaluable help, and
interfere seriously with the success of his
work.

How great the need of a praying church to
help move forward the preaching of the Word
of the Lord! Both pew and pulpit are jointly
concerned in this preaching business. It is a
copartnership. The two go hand in hand. One
must help the other; one can hinder the other.
Both must work in perfect accord. Otherwise,

Chapter Ten

The Preacher's Cry: "Pray for Us!"

That the true apostolic preacher must have the prayers of others—good people—to give to his ministry its full quota of success, Paul is a preeminent example. He asked, he coveted, he pleaded in an impassioned way for the help of all God's saints. He knew that in the spiritual realm as elsewhere, in union there is strength; that the consecration and aggregation of faith, desire, and prayer increased the volume of spiritual force until it became overwhelming and irresistible in its power. Units of prayer combined, like drops of water, make an ocean that defies resistance.

—E. M. Bounds

To what extent does praying for the preacher help preaching? It helps him personally and officially. It helps him to maintain a righteous life; it helps him in preparing his message; and it helps the Word he preaches to run to its appointed goal, unhindered and unhampered.

A praying church creates a spiritual atmosphere most favorable to preaching. What preacher who knows anything about the real work of preaching doubts the veracity of this statement? The spirit of prayer in a congregation produces an atmosphere supercharged with the Spirit of the Highest, removes obstacles, and gives the Word of the Lord the right-of-way. The very attitude of such a congregation constitutes an environment most encouraging and favorable to preaching. It renders preaching an easy task; it enables the Word to run quickly and without friction, propelled by the warmth of souls engaged in prayer.

People in the pew given to praying for the preacher, are like the poles that hold up the wires along which the electric current runs. They are not the power, nor are they the specific agents in making the Word of the Lord effective. But they hold up the wires along which the divine power runs to the hearts of men. They give liberty to the preacher and keep him from being hampered. They make conditions favorable for the preaching of the Gospel.

Many preachers have had much experience and know the truth of these statements. Yet, how hard they have found it to preach in some places! This was because they had no "door of utterance" (Col. 4:3) and were hampered in their delivery, there appearing no response whatsoever to their appeals. On the other hand, at other times thought flowed easily, words came freely, and there was no failure in speaking. The preacher "had liberty," as the old men say.

The preaching of the Word to a prayerless congregation falls at the very feet of the preacher. It has no traveling force; it stops because the atmosphere is cold, unsympathetic, and unfavorable to its running to the hearts of men and women. There is nothing to help it along. Just as some prayers never rise above the head of the one who prays, so the preaching of some preachers goes no farther than the front of the pulpit from which it is delivered. It takes prayer in the pulpit and prayer in the pew to make preaching arresting, life-giving, and soul-saving.

The Word of God is inseparably linked with prayer. The two are joined together, twins from birth and twins through life. The apostles found themselves absorbed by the sacred and pressing duty of distributing the alms of the church, until time was not left for them to pray. They directed that other men be appointed to do this task so that they would be better able to give themselves continually to prayer and to the ministry of the Word.

Likewise, the church's prayer for the preacher is also inseparably joined to preaching. A praying church is an invaluable help to the faithful preacher. The Word of the Lord runs in such a church, and it is glorified by the saving of sinners, by the reclaiming of backsliders, and by the sanctifying of believers. Paul connected the Word of God closely to prayer in writing to Timothy:

> *For every creature of God is good, and nothing to be refused, if it be received with thanksgiving: For it is sanctified by the word of God and prayer.*
> *(1 Tim. 4:4–5)*

And so the Word of the Lord depends on prayer for its rapid spread and for its full, glorious success.

Paul indicated that prayer transforms the ills that come to the preacher: "For I know that this shall turn to my salvation through your prayer, and the supply of the Spirit of Jesus Christ" (Phil. 1:19). It was through their prayers that these benefits would come to him. So, it is through the prayers of a church that the pastor will be the beneficiary of large spiritual things.

In the epistle to the Hebrews, Paul asked the Hebrew Christians to pray for him. He based his request on the grave and eternal responsibilities of the office of a preacher:

> *Obey them that have the rule over you, and submit yourselves: for they watch for your souls, as they that must give account, that they may do it with joy, and not with grief: for that is unprofitable for you. Pray for us: for we trust we have a good conscience, in all things willing to live honestly.*   *(Heb. 13:17–18)*

How little the church understands the fearful responsibility attached to the office and work of the ministry! "For they watch for your souls, as they that must give account." Preachers are God's watchmen, appointed to warn when danger is near. They are God's messengers, sent to rebuke, reprove, and exhort with all long-suffering. They are ordained as shepherds to protect the sheep against devouring wolves. How responsible is their position! And they are to give account to God for their work; they are to face a day of reckoning. How they need the prayers of those to whom they minister! And who should be more ready to do this praying than God's people, His own church, those who are presumably in harmony with the minister and his all-important work, divine in its origin?

Among the last messages of Jesus to His disciples are those found in the fourteenth, fifteenth, and sixteenth chapters of John's gospel. In the fourteenth, as well as in the others, are some very specific teachings about prayer, designed for the disciples' help and encouragement in their future work. We must never forget that these last discourses of Jesus Christ were given to disciples alone, away from the busy crowds, and seem primarily intended for them in their public ministry. In reality, they were words spoken to preachers, for these eleven men were to be the first preachers of the new dispensation.

With this thought in mind, we are able to see the tremendous importance given to prayer by our Lord. We can see the high place He gave it in the lifework of preachers, not only preachers in His day, but also preachers in future generations.

First, our Lord proposes that He will pray for these disciples that the Father might send them another Comforter, "even the Spirit of truth, whom the world cannot receive" (John 14:17). He preceded this statement by a direct command to them to pray, to pray for anything, with the assurance that they would receive what they asked for. (See John 14:13–14.)

If, therefore, there was value in their own praying and in our Lord's interceding for them, then, of course, it would be worthwhile in the future for their people to pray for them. It is no wonder, then, that the apostle Paul took the key from our Lord; several times he broke out with the urgent exhortation, "Pray for us" (1 Thess. 5:25; 2 Thess. 3:1).

True praying done by the laymen helps in many ways, but in one particular way. It very much helps the preacher to be brave and true. Read Paul's request to the Ephesians:

> *Praying always with all prayer and supplication in the Spirit, and watching thereunto with all perseverance and supplication for all saints; And for me, that utterance may be given unto me, that I may open my mouth boldly, to make known the mystery of the gospel, For which I am an ambassador in bonds: that therein I may speak boldly, as I ought to speak.   (Eph. 6:18–20)*

We do not know the extent to which the prayers of the church helped Paul be bold and true. But, it is unquestionable that through the prayers of the Christians at Ephesus, Colossae, and Thessalonica, he received much aid in preaching the Word. He would have been deprived of this aid had these churches not prayed for him. Likewise, in modern times the gift of ready and effective preaching has been bestowed upon a preacher through the prayers of the church.

The apostle Paul did not desire to fall short of that most important quality in a preacher of the Gospel, namely, boldness. He was no coward or chameleon or man-pleaser, but still he needed prayer. Prayer would give him courage to declare the whole truth of God. Prayer would keep him from fearing men and declaring the truth in an apologetic, hesitating way. He desired to remove himself as far as possible from an attitude of fear. His constant desire and effort was to declare the Gospel with freedom and consecrated boldness. "That I may open my mouth boldly, to make known the mystery of the gospel...that therein I may speak boldly, as I ought to speak" (Eph. 6:19–20). It would appear that, at times, he was really afraid that he might exhibit cowardice or be affected by the fear of man. But to speak boldly was his great desire.

This is a day that has urgent need for people from the mold of the great apostle— people of courage, brave and true. We need people who are not swayed by the fear of man. We need people who are not reduced to silence or apology by the dread of consequences. One way to secure these people is for the pew to engage in earnest prayer for the preachers.

In Paul's word to the Ephesian elders, given when on his way to Jerusalem, Paul cleared himself from the charge of blood-guiltiness, in that he had not failed to declare the whole counsel of God to them (Acts 20:26–27). To the Philippian believers, also, he said that through their prayers he would prove to be neither ashamed nor afraid (Phil 1:19–20).

Nothing, perhaps, can be more detrimental to the advancement of the kingdom of God than a timid or doubtful statement of revealed truth. The man who states only half of what he believes is the same as the man who states all but only half believes. No coward can preach the Gospel and declare the whole counsel of God. To do that, a man must be ready to do battle, not from passion, but from deep conviction, strong conscience, and complete courage. Faith is in the custody of a gallant heart; timidity always surrenders to a brave spirit.

Paul prayed, and prevailed on others to pray, that he might be a man of resolute courage, brave enough to do everything but sin. The result of this mutual praying is that history has no finer example of courage in a minister of Jesus Christ than that displayed in the life of the apostle Paul. He stands in the premier position as a fearless, uncompromising, God-fearing preacher of the Gospel.

God seems to have taken great pains with His prophets of old to save them from fear while they were delivering His messages to mankind. He sought in every way to safeguard His spokesmen from the fear of man. By means of command, reasoning, and encouragement, He sought to render them fearless and true to their high calling.

One of the besetting temptations of a preacher is the fear of man. Unfortunately, not a few surrender to this fear. Either they remain silent at times when they should be boldly eloquent, or they deliver a stern mandate softened with smooth words. "The fear of man bringeth a snare" (Prov. 29:25). With this sore temptation, Satan often assails the preacher of the Word, and there are few who have not felt the force of this temptation. It is the duty of ministers of the Gospel to face this temptation with resolute courage, to steel themselves against it, and, if need be, to trample it underfoot. To this important end, the preacher should be prayed for by his church. He needs deliverance from fear, and prayer can drive fear away and free his soul from its bondage.

In the seventeenth chapter of the book of Exodus, we have a striking picture of the preacher's need for prayer and for what a people's prayers can do for him. Israel and Amalek were in battle, and the contest was severe and close. Moses stood on top of the hill and held up his rod, the symbol of power and victory. As long as Moses held up the rod, Israel prevailed, but when he let down the rod, Amalek prevailed. The outcome of the battle was at stake. Aaron and Hur came to the rescue, and when Moses' hands were heavy, these two men "stayed up his hands...until the going down of the sun. And Joshua discomfited Amalek and his people" (Exod. 17:12–13).

This incident is a striking illustration of how a people may sustain their preacher by prayer. It further illustrates how victory comes when the people pray for their preacher.

Some of the Lord's very best men in Old Testament times had to be encouraged by almighty God not to be afraid. Moses himself was not free from the fear that harasses and compromises a leader. God told him, in these words, to go to Pharaoh: "Come now therefore, and I will send thee unto Pharaoh, that thou mayest bring forth my people the children of Israel out of Egypt" (Exod. 3:10). But Moses, largely through fear, began to offer objections and excuses for not going. Finally, God became angry with him and said that He would send Aaron along to do the talking, for Moses had insisted that he was "slow of speech, and of a slow tongue" (Exod. 4:10). But the fact was, Moses was afraid of the face of Pharaoh. It took God some time to circumvent his fears and nerve him to face the Egyptian monarch and deliver God's message to him.

Joshua, too, the successor of Moses and a man seemingly courageous, needed to be fortified by God against fear, lest he should shrink from duty and be reduced to discouragement and timidity. God said to him,

> *Have not I commanded thee? Be strong and of a good courage; be not afraid, neither be thou dismayed: for the LORD thy God is with thee whithersoever thou goest.*   *(Josh. 1:9)*

Jeremiah, a good and true man, was sorely tempted to fear. He had to be warned and strengthened, lest he should prove false to his charge. When God ordained him to be a prophet to the nations, Jeremiah began to excuse himself on the ground that he could not speak, saying, "I am a child" (Jer. 1:6). Therefore, the Lord had to safeguard him from the temptation of fear so that he might not prove faithless. God said to His servant,

> *Thou therefore gird up thy loins, and arise, and speak unto them all that I*

command thee: be not dismayed at their
faces, lest I confound thee before them.
> (Jer. 1:17)

Since these great men of old were so beset with this temptation and disposed to shrink from duty, we need not be surprised that preachers of our own day are found in a similar case. The Devil is the same in all ages, and human nature has not undergone any change. How needful, then, that we pray for the leaders of our Israel, especially that they may receive the gift of boldness and speak the Word of God with courage.

No wonder Paul insisted so vigorously that the believers pray for him. Prayer would give him an open door to preach, deliverance from the fear of man, and holy boldness in preaching the Word.

The challenge and demand of the world in our own day is that Christianity be made practical. The demand is for precepts to be expressed in practice, for principles to be brought down from the realm of the ideal to the levels of everyday life. This can be done only by praying men who, being much in harmony with their ministers, will not cease to bear them up in their prayers before God.

All alone, a preacher cannot meet the demands made upon him, any more than the vine can bear grapes without branches. The men who sit in the pews are to be the fruit-bearing ones. They are to translate the "ideal" of the pulpit into the "real" of daily life and action. But they will not do it, they cannot do it, if they are not devoted to God and given to much prayer. Devotion to God and devotion to prayer are one and the same thing.

Chapter Eleven

Modern Examples
of Prayer

When the dragon-fly rends his husk and harnesses himself in a clean plate of sapphire mail, his is a pilgrimage of one or two sunny days over the fields and pastures wet with dew, yet nothing can exceed the marvelous beauty in which he is decked. No flowers on earth have a richer blue than the pure colour of his cuirass. So is it in the high spiritual sphere. The most complete spiritual loveliness may be obtained in the shortest time, and the stripling may die a hundred years old, in character and grace.

—History of David Brainerd

God has not confined Himself to Bible days in showing what can be done through prayer. In modern times, also, He is seen to be the same prayer-hearing God as before. Even in these latter days He has not left Himself without witness. Religious biographies and church history alike furnish us with many noble examples and striking illustrations of prayer. These examples show us prayer's necessity, its worth, and its fruits.

All these examples also encourage the faith of God's saints and urge them on to more and better praying. God has not confined Himself to Bible times in using praying people to further His cause on earth. He has placed Himself under obligation to answer our prayers just as much as He did the saints of old. A selection from these praying saints of modern times will show us how they valued prayer, what it meant to them, and what it meant to God.

Take, for example, Samuel Rutherford, a Scottish preacher, exiled to the north of Scotland, forbidden to preach, and banished from his home and pastoral charge. Rutherford lived between 1600 and 1661. He was a member of the Westminster Assembly, principal of New College, and rector of St. Andrews' University. He is said to have been one of the most moving and affectionate preachers of his time, or, perhaps, of any age of the church. Men said of him, "He is always praying." Concerning his and his wife's praying, one wrote,

He who had heard them either pray
or speak, might have learned to bemoan
his ignorance. Oh, how many times have

I been convinced by observing them of the evil of insincerity before God and unsavoriness in discourse! He so prayed for his people that he himself says, "There I wrestled with the Angel and prevailed." (See Genesis 32:24–28.)

Rutherford was ordered to appear before Parliament to answer the charge of high treason, even though he was a man of scholarly attainments and rare genius. At times he was depressed and gloomy, especially when he was first silenced and banished from preaching, for there were many murmurings and charges against him. But his losses and crosses were so sanctified that Christ became more and more to him. Marvelous are his statements of his estimation of Christ. This devoted man of prayer wrote many letters during his exile to preachers, to state officers, to lords temporal and spiritual, to honorable and holy men, to honorable and holy women. These were precious letters, all breathing an intense devotion to Christ and all born of great devotion to prayer.

Ardor and panting after God have been characteristics of great souls in all ages of the church, and Samuel Rutherford was a striking example of this fact. He showed that he who always prays will be enveloped in devotion and will be joined to Christ in bonds of holy union.

Then there was Henry Martyn—scholar, saint, missionary, and apostle to India. Martyn was born on February 18, 1781 and sailed for India on August 31, 1805. He died at Tokai, Persia, October 16, 1812. Here is part of what he said about himself while a missionary:

> What a knowledge of man and acquaintance with the Scriptures, and what communion with God and study of my own heart ought to prepare me for the awful work of a messenger from God on business of the soul.

Someone said of this consecrated missionary:

> Oh, to be able to emulate his excellencies, his elevation of piety, his diligence, his superiority to the world, his love for souls, his anxiety to improve on all occasions to do souls good, his insight into the mystery of Christ, and his heavenly temper! These are the secrets of the wonderful impression he made in India.

It is interesting and profitable to note some of the things that Martyn records in his ~ry. Here is an example:

The ways of wisdom appear more sweet and reasonable than ever, and the world more insipid and vexatious. The chief thing I mourn over is my want of power, and lack of fervour in secret prayer, especially when attempting to plead for the heathen. Warmth does not increase within me in proportion to my light.

If Henry Martyn, so devoted, ardent, and prayerful, lamented his lack of power and fervor in prayer, how our cold and feeble praying ought to lower us into the very dust! Alas, how rare are such praying men in the church of our own day!

Again, I quote an entry from his diary. He had been quite ill, but he had recovered, and he was filled with thankfulness because it had pleased God to restore him to life and health again.

Not that I have yet recovered my former strength, but I consider myself sufficiently restored to prosecute my journey. My daily prayer is that my late chastisement may have its intended effect and make me, all the rest of my days, more humble and less self-confident.

Self-confidence has often led me
down fearful lengths and would, without God's gracious interference, prove
my endless perdition. I seem to be made
to feel this evil of my heart more than
any other at this time. In prayer, or
when I write or converse on the subject,
Christ appears to me my life and my
strength; but at other times I am
thoughtless and bold, as if I had all life
and strength in myself. Such neglects
on our part are a diminution of our joys.

Among the last entries in this consecrated missionary's journal we find the following:

In solitude, I sat in the orchard and
thought, with sweet comfort and peace,
of my God—my Company, my Friend,
my Comforter. Oh, when shall time give
place to eternity!

Note the words "in solitude." Away from
the busy haunts of men, in a lonely place, like
his Lord, he went out to meditate and pray.

Brief as this summary is, it suffices to
show how fully and faithfully Henry Martyn
exercised his ministry of prayer. The following may well serve to end our portrayal of
him:

By daily weighing the Scriptures, with prayer, he waxed riper and riper in his ministry. Prayer and the Holy Scriptures were those wells of salvation out of which he drew daily the living water for his thirsty immortal soul. Truly may it be said of him, he prayed "always with all prayer and supplication in the Spirit, and watch[ed] thereunto with all perseverance" (Eph. 6:18).

David Brainerd, the missionary to the Indians, is a remarkable example of a praying man of God. Robert Hale said this about him:

Such invincible patience and self-denial; such profound humility, exquisite prudence, indefatigable industry; such devotedness to God, or rather such absorption of the whole soul in zeal for the divine glory and the salvation of men, is scarcely to be paralleled since the age of the Apostles. Such was the intense ardour of his mind that it seems to have diffused the spirit of a martyr over the common incidents of his life.

Dr. A. J. Gordon spoke thus of Brainerd:

In passing through Northampton, Massachusetts, I went into the old cemetery, swept off the snow that lay on the top of the slab, and I read these simple words:

"Sacred to the memory of David Brainerd, the faithful and devoted missionary to the Susquehanna, Delaware and Stockbridge Indians of America, who died in this town, October 8th, 1747."

That was all there was on the slab. Now that great man did his greatest work by prayer. He was in the depths of those forests alone, unable to speak the language of the Indians, but he spent whole days literally in prayer.

What was he praying for? He knew he could not reach these savages, for he did not understand their language. If he wanted to speak at all, he must find somebody who could vaguely interpret his thought. Therefore he knew that anything he could do must be absolutely dependent upon God. So he spent whole days in praying, simply that the power of the Holy Ghost might come upon him so unmistakably that these people would not be able to stand before him.

What was his answer? Once he preached through a drunken interpreter, a man so intoxicated that he could hardly stand up. This was the best he could do. Yet scores were converted through that sermon. We can account for it only that it was the tremendous power of God behind him.

Now this man prayed in secret in the forest. A little while afterward, William Carey read about his life, and by its impulse he went to India. Payson read it as a young man, over twenty years old, and he said that he had never been so impressed by anything in his life as by the story of Brainerd. Murray McCheyne read it, and he likewise was impressed by it.

But all I want is simply to enforce this thought, that the hidden life, a life whose days are spent in communion with God, in trying to reach the source of power, is the life that moves the world. Those living such lives may be soon forgotten. There may be no one to speak a eulogy over them when they are dead. The great world may take no account of them. But by and by, the great moving current of their lives will begin to tell, as in the case of this young man, who died at about thirty years of age. The missionary spirit of this nineteenth century is more due to the prayers and consecration of this one man than to any other one.

So I say. And yet the most remarkable thing is that Jonathan Edwards, who watched over him all those months while he was slowly dying of consumption, should also say: "I praise God that it was in His Providence that he should die in my house, that I might hear his prayers, and that I might witness his consecration, and that I might be inspired by his example."

When Jonathan Edwards wrote that great appeal to Christendom to unite in prayer for the conversion of the world, which has been the trumpet call of modern missions, undoubtedly it was inspired by this dying missionary.

John Wesley bore this testimony about David Brainerd's spirit:

I preached and afterward made a collection for the Indian schools in America. A large sum of money is now collected. But will money convert heathens? Find preachers of David Brainerd's spirit, and nothing can stand before them. But without this, what will gold or silver do? No more than lead or iron.

Some selections from Brainerd's diary will value to show what manner of man he was:

My soul felt a pleasing yet painful concern, lest I should spend some moments without God. Oh, may I always live to God! In the evening I was visited by some friends, and we spent the time in prayer, and such conversation as tended to edification. It was a comfortable season to my soul. I felt an ardent desire to spend every moment with God.

God is unspeakably gracious to me continually. In time past, He has given me inexpressible sweetness in the performance of duty. Frequently my soul has enjoyed much of God, but has been ready to say, "Lord, it is good to be here," and so indulge sloth while I have lived on the sweetness of my feelings. But of late God has been pleased to keep my soul hungry almost continually, so that I have been filled with a kind of pleasing pain. When I really enjoy God, I feel my desires of Him the more insatiable, and my thirstings after holiness the more unquenchable.

Oh, that I may feel this continual hunger, and not be retarded, but rather animated, by every cluster from Canaan, to reach forward in the narrow way, for the full enjoyment and possession of the heavenly inheritance! Oh, may I never loiter in my heavenly journey!

It seems as if such an unholy wretch as I never could arrive at that blessedness, to be holy as God is holy. At noon I longed for sanctification and conformity to God. Oh, that is the one thing, the all!

Toward night I enjoyed much sweetness in secret prayer, so that my soul longed for an arrival in the heavenly country, the blessed paradise of God.

If someone should ask about the secret of David Brainerd's heavenly spirit, his deep consecration, and his exalted spiritual state, the answer can be found in the last sentence of the preceding quote. He was given to "much...secret prayer," and he was so close to God in his life and spirit that prayer brought much sweetness to his inner soul.

We have cited the foregoing cases to illustrate the fundamental fact that God's great servants are devoted to the ministry of prayer. They are God's agents on earth who serve Him in this way, and they carry on His work by this holy means.

Louis Harms was born in Hanover in 1809. There came a time when he was powerfully convicted of sin. He said, "I have never known what fear was. But when I came to the knowledge of my sins, I quaked before the wrath of God, so that my limbs trembled." He was mightily converted to God by reading the Bible.

Rationalism, a dead orthodoxy, and worldliness blinded the multitudes in Hermansburgh, the town where he lived. His father, a Lutheran minister, died, and Harms became his successor. He began with all the energy of his soul to work for Christ and to develop a church of a pure, strong type. The fruit was soon evident. There was a quickening on every hand; attendance at public services increased; reverence for the Bible grew; conversation about sacred things revived. Meanwhile, infidelity, worldliness, and dead orthodoxy vanished like a passing cloud.

Harms proclaimed a conscious and present Christ, the Comforter, in the full energy of His mission, which is the revival of apostolic piety and power. The entire neighborhood began to attend church regularly; the Sabbath was restored to its sanctity and hallowed with strict devotion; homes began to have family devotions; and when the noon bell sounded, every head was bowed in prayer. In a very short time the whole aspect of the town was entirely changed.

The revival in Hermansburgh was essentially a prayer revival. It was brought about by prayer and yielded fruits of prayer in a rich and abundant harvest.

William Carvosso, an old-time Methodist leader, was one of the best examples in modern times of what the religious life of Christians was probably like in the apostolic age. He was a prayer leader, a class leader, a steward, and a trustee, but he never aspired to be a preacher. Yet, a preacher he was of the very first quality, and he was a master in the art and science of soul-saving. He was a singular example of a man learning the simplest rudiments late in life. Up until the age of sixty-five, he had never written a single sentence. Yet, he later wrote letters that would make volumes, and he wrote a book that was regarded as a spiritual classic in the great worldwide Methodist church.

Not a page nor a letter, it is believed, was ever written by him on any other subject but religion. Here are some of his brief statements, which give us an insight into his religious character. "I want to be more like Jesus." "My soul thirsteth for Thee, O God." "I see nothing will do, O God, but being continually filled with Thy presence and glory."

This was the continual cry of his inner soul, and this was the strong inward impulse that moved the outward man. One time he exclaimed, "Glory to God! This is a morning without a cloud." Cloudless days were native to his sunny religion and his joyful spirit. Continual prayer and turning all conversation toward Christ in all company and in every home, was the law he always followed.

On the anniversary of his spiritual birth, he remembered his salvation experience with great joyousness of spirit, and he broke forth:

> Blessed be Thy name, O God! The last has been the best of the whole. I may say with Bunyan, "I have got into that land where the sun shines night and day." I thank Thee, O my God, for this heaven, this element of love and joy, in which my soul now lives.

Here is a sample of Carvosso's spiritual experiences, of which he had many:

> I have sometimes had seasons of remarkable visitation from the presence of the Lord. I well remember one night when in bed being so filled, so overpowered with the glory of God, that had there been a thousand suns shining at noonday, the brightness of that divine glory would have eclipsed the whole. I was constrained to shout aloud for joy. It was the overwhelming power of saving grace. Now it was that I again received the impress of the seal and the

earnest of the Spirit in my heart. Beholding as in a glass the glory of the Lord, I was changed into the same image from glory to glory by the Spirit of the Lord (2 Cor. 3:18). Language fails in giving but a faint description of what I there experienced. I can never forget it in time nor to all eternity.

Many years before I was sealed by the Spirit in a somewhat similar manner. While walking out one day, I was drawn to turn aside on the public road, and under the canopy of the skies, I was moved to kneel down to pray. I had not long been praying with God before I was so visited from Him that I was overpowered by the divine glory, and I shouted till I could be heard at a distance. It was a weight of glory that I seemed incapable of bearing in the body, and therefore I cried out, perhaps unwisely, "Lord, stay Thy hand." In this glorious baptism these words came to my heart with indescribable power: "I have sealed thee unto the day of redemption." (See Ephesians 4:30.)

Oh, I long to be filled more with God! Lord, stir me up more in earnest. I want to be more like Jesus. I see that nothing will do but being continually filled with the divine presence and

glory. I know all that Thou hast is mine,
but I want to feel a close union. Lord,
increase my faith.

Such was William Carvosso—a man whose
life was saturated with the spirit of prayer,
who lived on his knees, so to speak, and who
belonged to that company of praying saints
that has blessed the earth.

Jonathan Edwards must be placed among
the praying saints—one whom God mightily
used through the instrumentality of prayer. As
in the instance of this great New Englander,
purity of heart should be ingrained in the very
foundation of every person who is a minister of
the Gospel. A sample of the statements of this
mighty man of God is here given in the form of
a resolution he wrote down:

> Resolved to exercise myself in this
> all my life long, viz., with the greatest
> openness to declare my ways to God,
> and to lay my soul open to God—all my
> sins, temptations, difficulties, sorrows,
> fears, hopes, desires, and everything
> and every circumstance.

We are not surprised, therefore, that the
result of such fervid and honest praying was to
lead him to record in his diary:

It was my continual strife day and night, and my constant inquiry, how I should be more holy, and live more holily. The heaven I desired was a heaven of holiness. I went on with my eager pursuit after more holiness and conformity to Christ.

The character and work of Jonathan Edwards exemplified a great truth: prayer is the activating agency in every truly God-ordered work and life. He himself gives some particulars about his life as a boy. He might well be called the "Isaiah of the Christian Dispensation." There were united in him great mental powers, ardent piety, and devotion to study; these were unequaled except by his devotion to God. Here is what he said about himself:

When a boy I used to pray five times a day in secret, and to spend much time in religious conversation with other boys. I used to meet with them to pray together. So it is God's will through His wonderful grace, that the prayers of His saints should be one great and principal means of carrying on the designs of Christ's kingdom in the world. Pray much for the ministers and the church of God.

Edwards used the great powers of his mind and heart to get God's people everywhere to unite in extraordinary prayer. His life, efforts, and character are an exemplification of his statement. He said,

> The heaven I desire is a heaven spent with God: an eternity spent in the presence of divine love, and in holy communion with Christ.

At another time he said,

> The soul of a true Christian appears like a little white flower in the spring of the year, low and humble on the ground, opening its bosom to receive the pleasant beams of the sun's glory, rejoicing as it were in a calm rapture, diffusing around a sweet fragrance, standing peacefully and lovingly in the midst of other flowers.

Again, he wrote,

> Once, having ridden out into the woods for my health, I alighted from my horse in a retired place, for my manner has been to walk for divine contemplation and prayer. I had a view, that for me was extraordinary, of the glory of

the Son of God as Mediator between God and man, and of His wonderful, great, full, pure, and sweet grace and love, and His meek and gentle condescension. This grace that seemed so calm and sweet, appeared also great above the heavens. The person of Christ appeared ineffably excellent with an excellency great enough to swallow up all thought and conception, which continued, as near as I can judge, about an hour. It kept me the greater part of the time in a flood of tears and weeping aloud. I felt an ardency of soul to be, what I know not otherwise how to express, emptied and annihilated, to lie in the dust; to be full of Christ alone, to love Him with my whole heart.

As it was with Jonathan Edwards, so it is with all great intercessors. They come into that holy, elect condition of mind and heart by a thorough self-dedication to God, and by periods of God's revelation to them, which make distinct, marked eras in their spiritual history. These eras are never to be forgotten. During these eras faith "mount[s] up with wings as eagles" (Isa. 40:31). The intercessor has a new and fuller vision of God; a stronger grasp of faith; a sweeter, clearer vision of all things heavenly and eternal; and a blessed intimacy with, and access to, God.

Chapter Twelve

More Modern Examples of Prayer

Edward Bounds did not merely pray well that he might write well about prayer. He prayed for long years upon subjects to which easy-going Christians rarely give a thought. He prayed for objects which men of less faith are ready to call impossible. Yet from these continued, solitary prayer-vigils, year by year there arose a gift of prayer-teaching equaled by few men. He wrote transcendently about prayer because he was transcendent in its practice. —C. L. Chilton, Jr.

Lady Maxwell was a contemporary of John Wesley, and she was a fruit of Methodism in its earlier phases. She was a woman of refinement, of culture, and of deep piety. Separating herself entirely from the world, she sought and found the deepest religious experience, and she was a woman fully set apart to God.

Her life was one of prayer, of complete consecration to God, of living to bless others. She was noted for her systematic habits of life, which entered into and controlled her religion. Her time was economized and ordered for God. She arose at four o'clock in the morning and attended preaching at five o'clock. After breakfast she held a family service. Then, from eleven to twelve o'clock she observed a season of intercessory prayer. The rest of the day was given to reading, visiting, and acts of benevolence. Her evenings were spent in reading. At night, before retiring, religious services were held for the family, which sometimes were spent in praising God for His mercies.

Rarely has God been served with more intelligence or out of a richer experience, a nobler zeal, or a greater nobility of soul. Strongly, spiritually, and ardently attached to Wesley's doctrine of entire dedication, she sought it with persistency and a never-flagging zeal. She obtained it by faith and prayer, and she illustrated it in a life as holy and as perfect as is given to mortals to reach. If Wesley's teaching of entire dedication had, today, models and teachers like Lady Maxwell of Edinburgh and John Fletcher of Madeley, it would not be so misunderstood. No, it would commend itself to the good and pure everywhere by holy lives, if not by its phraseology.

Lady Maxwell's diary yields some rich counsel for secret prayer, holy experience, and consecrated living. One of the entries reads as follows:

> Of late I feel painfully convinced that I do not pray enough. Lord, give me the spirit of prayer and of supplication. Oh, what a cause of thankfulness it is that we have a gracious God to whom to go on all occasions! Use and enjoy this privilege and you can never be miserable. Who gives thanks for this royal privilege? It puts God in everything, His wisdom, power, control and safety. Oh, what an unspeakable privilege is prayer! Let us give thanks for it. I do not prove all the power of prayer that I wish.

Thus, we see that the remedy for non-praying is *praying*. The cure for little praying is more praying. Praying can procure all things necessary for our good.

For this excellent woman, praying embraced everything and included everything. To one of her most intimate friends she wrote,

> I wish I could provide you with a proper maid, but it is a difficult matter. You have my prayers for it, and if I hear of one I will let you know.

So small a matter as a friend's need for a maid was not too small for her to take to God in prayer.

In the same letter she tells her friend that she wants "more faith. Cry mightily for it, and stir up the gift of God that is in you." (See 2 Timothy 1:6.)

Whether the need was a small, secular thing like a servant, or a great spiritual grace, prayer was the means to attain that end and supply that need. She wrote to a dear correspondent,

> There is nothing so hurtful to the nervous system as anxiety. It preys upon the vitals and weakens the whole frame, and what is more than all, it grieves the Holy Spirit.

Her remedy, again, for a common evil, was prayer.

How prayer lifts the burden of care by bringing in God to relieve and possess and hold!

The apostle said,

> *Be careful for nothing; but in every thing by prayer and supplication with thanksgiving let your requests be made known unto God. And the peace of God, which*

*passeth all understanding, shall keep
your hearts and minds through Christ
Jesus.* (Phil. 4:6–7)

These verses tell us that God keeps and
protects us. Picture a besieged and distressed
garrison, unable to protect the fort from at-
tacking enemies, when suddenly strong rein-
forcements come pouring in. Into the heart
oppressed, distracted, and discouraged, true
prayer brings God, who holds it in perfect
peace and perfect safety. Lady Maxwell fully
understood this truth, not only theoretically,
but, even better, experientially.

Christ Jesus is the only cure for needless
care and overanxiety of soul, and we secure
God, His presence, and His peace by prayer.
Care is so natural and so strong that no one
but God can drive it out. It takes the presence
and personality of God Himself to expel the
care and to enthrone quietness and peace.
When Christ comes in with His peace, all
tormenting fears leave. Trepidation and vex-
ing anxieties surrender to Christ's reign of
peace, and all disturbing elements depart.

Anxious thought and care assault the
soul, and feebleness, faintness, and cowardice
are within. Prayer reinforces with God's
peace, and the heart is kept by Him. "Thou
wilt keep him in perfect peace, whose mind is

stayed on thee" (Isa. 26:3). All now is safety, quietness, and assurance. "The work of righteousness shall be peace; and the effect of righteousness quietness and assurance for ever" (Isa. 32:17).

But to ensure this great peace, prayer must pass into strenuous, insistent, personal supplication, and thanksgiving must bloom into full flower. Our exposed condition of heart must be brought to the knowledge of God "by prayer and supplication with thanksgiving" (Phil. 4:6). The peace of God will keep the heart and thoughts fixed and fearless. Peace—deep, exhaustless, wide, flowing like a river—will come in.

Referring again to Lady Maxwell, we remember her words:

> God is daily teaching me more simplicity of spirit, and He makes me willing to receive all as His unmerited gift. He is teaching me to call on Him for everything I need, as I need it, and He supplies my wants according to existing needs. But I have certainly felt more of it this last eighteen months than in former periods. I wish to "pray without ceasing" (1 Thess. 5:17). I see the necessity of praying always, and not fainting (Luke 18:1).

Again, we recall her words: "I wish to be much in prayer. I greatly need it. The prayer of faith shuts or opens heaven. Come, Lord, and turn my captivity." If we felt the need of prayer as this saintly woman did, we could be like her in her saintly ascension. Prayer truly shuts or opens heaven. Oh, for a quality of faith that would test to the uttermost the power of prayer!

Lady Maxwell uttered a great truth when she said,

> When God is at work, either among a people or in the heart of an individual, the adversary of souls is peculiarly at work also. A belief of the former should prevent discouragement, and a fear of the latter should stir us up to much prayer. Oh, the power of faithful prayer! I live by prayer! May you prove its sovereign efficacy in every difficult case.

A record among Lady Maxwell's writings shows us that in prayer and meditation she obtained enlarged views of the full salvation of God. What is thus discovered in prayer, faith goes out after, and according to faith's strength are its returns.

> I daily feel the need of the precious blood of sprinkling [she said] and dwell

continually under its influence, and most sensibly feel its sovereign efficacy. It is by momentary faith in this blood alone that I am saved from sin. Prayer is my chief employ.

If this last statement, "Prayer is my chief employ," had ever been true of all of God's people, this world would have been by this time quite another world; and God's glory, instead of being dim, shadowy, and only in spots, would now shine with universal and unrivaled brilliance and power.

Here is another record of her fervent and faithful praying: "Lately, I have been favoured with a more ardent spirit of praying than almost ever formerly."

We need to study the words "favoured with a more ardent spirit of praying," for they are pregnant words. The spirit of prayer, the ardent spirit of prayer, and the more ardent spirit of prayer—all these are of God. They are given in answer to prayer. The spirit of prayer and the more ardent spirit are the result of fervent, persistent, secret prayer.

At another time Lady Maxwell declared that secret prayer was the means whereby she derived the greatest spiritual benefit.

I do indeed prove it to be an especial privilege. I could not live without it, though I do not always find comfort in it. I still ardently desire an enlarged sphere of usefulness, and find it comfortable to embrace the opportunities afforded me.

An "enlarged sphere of usefulness" is certainly a proper theme of intense prayer, but that prayer must always be accompanied by an embracing of the opportunities one already has.

Many pages could be filled with extracts from Lady Maxwell's diary about the vital importance and the nature of prayer, but we must conclude. For many years she was in fervent supplication for a larger sphere of usefulness, but all these years of ardent praying may be condensed into one paragraph:

My whole soul has been thirsting after a larger sphere of action [she said] agreeably to the promises of a faithful God. For these few last weeks I have been led to plead earnestly for more holiness. Lord, give me both, that I may praise Thee.

These two things—more work and more holiness—must go together. They are one, and they are not to be separated. The desire for a larger field of work without the accompanying desire for more consecration is perilous, and it may be supremely selfish, the offspring of spiritual pride.

John Fletcher, also a contemporary of John Wesley, was intimately associated with this founder of Methodism. Fletcher was a scholar of courtesy and refinement; a strong, original thinker; a speaker of simple eloquence and truth. What qualified him as a spiritual leader was his exceedingly great faith in God, his nearness to God, and his perfect assurance of a dear, unquestioned relationship with his Lord. Fletcher had profound convictions about the truth of God, possessed a perpetual communion with his Savior, and was humble in his knowledge of God. He was a man of deep spiritual insight into the things of God, and his thorough earnestness, his truth, and his consecration marked him as a man of God. He was well equipped to be a leader in the church.

Unceasing prayer was the sign and secret of Fletcher's sainthood, as well as its power and influence. His whole life was one of prayer. So intently was his mind fixed on God that he sometimes said, "I would not rise from my seat without lifting up my heart to God." A friend related the fact that whenever they met, Fletcher's first greeting was, "Do I meet you praying?" If they were talking about theology, in the midst of it he would stop abruptly and say, "Where are our hearts now?" If the misconduct of any person who was absent was mentioned, he would say, "Let us pray for him."

The very walls of his room, so it was said, were stained by the breath of his prayers. Spiritually, Madeley was a dreary, desolate desert when he went to live there, but it was so revolutionized by his prayers that it bloomed and blossomed like the garden of the Lord. A friend of his thus wrote of Fletcher:

> Many of us have at times gone with him aside, and there we would continue for two or three hours, wrestling like Jacob for the blessing, praying one after another. And I have seen him on these occasions so filled with the love of God that he could contain no more, but would cry out, "O my God, withhold Thy hand or the vessel will burst!" His whole life was a life of prayer.

John Foster, a man of exalted piety and deep devotion to God, said this about prayer while on his deathbed:

> "Pray without ceasing" (1 Thess. 5:17) has been the sentence repeating

itself in my silent thoughts, and I am sure that it will be, it must be, my practice till the last conscious hour of my life. Oh, why was it not my practice throughout that long, indolent, inanimate half century past! I often think mournfully of the difference it would have made in me. Now there remains so little time for a genuine, effective spiritual life.

The Reformation of the fifteenth century owes its origin to prayer. In all of Martin Luther's lifework—its beginning, continuance, and ending—he was devoted to prayer. The secret of his extraordinary activity is found in this statement: "I have so much work to do that I cannot get along without giving three hours daily of my best time to prayer." Another one of his sayings was, "It takes meditation and prayer to make a clergyman." His everyday motto was, "He that has prayed well, has studied well."

Another time he confessed his lack by saying, "I was short and superficial in prayer this morning." How often is this the case with us! Remember that the source of decline in religion and the proof of decline in a Christian life is found right here, in "short and superficial" praying. Such praying foretells and causes coldness between us and God.

More Modern Examples of Prayer

William Wilberforce once said of himself,

> I have been keeping too late hours,
> and hence have had but a hurried half
> hour to myself. I am lean and cold and
> hard. I had better allow more time, say
> two hours, or an hour-and-a-half, daily
> to religious exercises.

A person must be very skillful and regular in long praying for his short prayers not to be superficial. Short prayers make shallow lives. Longer praying would work like magic in many a decayed spiritual life. A holy life would not be so difficult and rare if our praying were not so brief, cold, and superficial.

George Müller, that remarkable man of such simple yet strong faith in God, was a man of prayer and Bible reading. He was the founder and promoter of the noted orphanage in England, which cared for hundreds of orphan children. He conducted the institution solely by faith and prayer. He never asked a man for anything, but he simply trusted in the providence of God, and it is a well-known fact that the orphans at the home never lacked any good thing. From his newsletter he always excluded money matters, and financial difficulties found no place in it. Nor would he mention the sums that had been given him, nor the names of those who had made contributions. He never spoke of his needs to others or asked for a donation.

The story of his life and the history of this orphanage read like a chapter from the Scriptures. The secret of his success is found in this simple statement made by him: "I went to my God and prayed diligently, and I received what I needed." That was the simple course that he pursued. There was nothing he insisted on with more earnestness than that, no matter what the expenses were or how suddenly they increased, he must not beg for anything. There was nothing that he told more excitedly than that he had prayed for every need he had ever had in his great work. His was a work of continuous and persevering praying, and he always confidently claimed that God had guided him throughout it all. His work was a proof of the power of simple faith, divine providence, answered prayer. A stronger proof cannot be found in church history or religious biography.

John Wesley, in writing to a friend one time, helped, urged, and prayed. Here are John Wesley's own words:

> Have you received a gleam of light from above, a spark of faith? If you have, let it not go! Hold fast by His grace that earnest of your inheritance.

Come just as you are, and come boldly to the throne of grace. You need not delay. Even now the bowels of Jesus yearn over you. What have you to do with tomorrow? I love you to-day. And how much more does He love you? "He pities still His wandering sheep, and longs to bring you to His fold." To-day hear His voice, the voice of Him that speaks as never man spake.

The seekings of Madame Guyon after God were sincere, and her yearnings were strong and earnest. She went to a devout Franciscan friar for advice and comfort. She stated her convictions and told him of her long and fruitless seeking. After she had finished speaking to him, the friar remained silent for some time, in inward meditation and prayer. Then he said to her,

Your efforts have been unsuccessful, because you have *sought without* what you can only *find within*. Accustom yourself to seek God in your heart, and you will not fail to find Him.

Charley G. Finney said this about prayer:

When God has specially promised the thing, we are bound to believe we shall receive it when we pray for it. You have no right to put in an "if," and say, "Lord, *if* it be Thy will, give me Thy Holy Spirit." This is to insult God. To put an "if" in God's promise when God has put none there, is tantamount to charging God with being insincere. It is like saying, "O God, if Thou art in earnest in making these promises, grant us the blessing we pray for."

We may fittingly conclude this book by quoting a word of Adoniram Judson's, the noted missionary to Burma. Speaking of the prevailing power of prayer, he said,

"Nothing is impossible," said one of the seven sages of Greece, "to industry." Let us change the word, "industry," to "persevering prayer," and the motto will be more Christian and more worthy of universal adoption. God loves importunate prayer so much that He will not give us much blessing without it. God says, "Behold, I will do a new thing; now it shall spring forth; shall ye not know it? I will even make a way in the wilderness, and rivers in the desert...This people have I formed for myself; they shall show forth my praise" (Isa. 43:19, 21).

Success for your Vision

Ross - Muro

1) purpose
2) passion
3) protential
4) planning
5) people -
6) persistence - breaks down Resistence
7) principles
8) prayer
   "Consulting your resource
   "Constant Communion with the
   Father"

barran
Toxic
Fertile

Test comes to Rate you

1) to show you what do know
2) what you don't know
3) where you weak
4) where your strong